CLASS

A GRAPHIC GUIDE

LAURA HARVEY SARAH LEANEY DANNY NOBLE

ICON

Published in the UK and the USA in 2022 by
Icon Books Ltd, Omnibus Business Centre,
39–41 North Road, London N7 9DP
email: info@iconbooks.net
www.iconbooks.com

Sold in the UK, Europe and Asia by
Faber & Faber Ltd, Bloomsbury House,
74-77 Great Russell Street,
London WC1B 3DA or their agents

Distributed in the UK, Europe and Asia by
Grantham Book Services
Trent Road, Grantham NG31 7XQ

Distributed in Australia and New Zealand by
Allen & Unwin Pty Ltd,
PO Box 8500, 83 Alexander Street,
Crows Nest, NSW 2065

Distributed in Canada by
Publishers Group Canada,
76 Stafford Street, Unit 300,
Toronto, Ontario M6J 2S1

Distributed in India by
Penguin Books India,
7th Floor, Infinity Tower – C, DLF Cyber City,
Gurgaon 122002, Haryana

Distributed in South Africa by
Jonathan Ball, Office B4, The District,
41 Sir Lowry Road,
Woodstock 7925

Distributed in the USA by
Publishers Group West,
1700 Fourth Street,
Berkeley, CA 94710

ISBN: 978-178578-691-4

Originating editor: Kiera Jamison

Printed and bound in Great Britain by Clays Ltd, Elcograf S.P.A.

INTRODUCING CLASS

Class can be found in many spheres of our lives, but it can be difficult to pin down. We often use other words and images to talk about class. When class is spoken about directly, it can have different meanings to different people. In this book, we will be thinking about class as:

- an idea to describe inequalities in society
- a category based on our job or income
- a group of people who are fighting for their rights
- a struggle over power
- an influence on our likes and dislikes
- a label shaping how we feel about ourselves and other people.

CLASS IS HARD TO DEFINE. WHEN WE SPEAK ABOUT CLASS, DO WE MEAN CLASS STRUCTURE, IDENTITY, CONSCIOUSNESS OR ACTION?*

SOCIOLOGIST BEVERLEY SKEGGS

Speech bubbles in this book aren't always direct quotes – they're often paraphrased to give a sense of each author's ideas, rather than their exact words.

This book will introduce you to different ways of understanding class. We will explore a range of theories about what class is and the broad effects it has, and we'll encourage you to think about class in your own life.

We hope to spark your interest, highlight examples of when class has been challenged and inspire you to think about how we can break down class inequality.

Thinking about class can help us to:
· see how resources are unfairly distributed
· question stereotypes
· notice and challenge unfairness
· find ways to stand up for each other
· reflect on how our lives are connected to others'.

4

All theories of class are developed in specific historical and social contexts, so they reflect the world as seen through the authors' eyes in that particular moment. Our own learning and research about class has been shaped by our social background. We have tried to disrupt dominant narratives of class by using critical perspectives to interrogate "classical" theories and our own ideas.

WESTERN THEORIES ABOUT CLASS HAVE DOMINATED THE NARRATIVE. THEY HAVE ALSO INFLUENCED HOW CLASS HAS BEEN "MEASURED" GLOBALLY.

IT'S IMPORTANT TO EXPLORE THESE THEORIES, AS THEY HAVE SHAPED KNOWLEDGE AND EXPERIENCES OF CLASS. WE'LL TALK EXPLICITLY ABOUT THE CONTEXT IN WHICH THESE WERE WRITTEN, AND THEIR IMPACTS ACROSS BORDERS.

DELVING INTO DIFFERENT ASPECTS OF CLASS REVEALS MORE WEBS OF INTERCONNECTED IDEAS AND HISTORIES. WE TRY TO POINT TO MULTIPLE PERSPECTIVES THROUGHOUT THE BOOK.

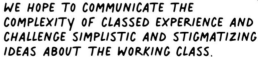

WE HOPE TO COMMUNICATE THE COMPLEXITY OF CLASSED EXPERIENCE AND CHALLENGE SIMPLISTIC AND STIGMATIZING IDEAS ABOUT THE WORKING CLASS.

ALTHOUGH THIS BOOK FOCUSES ON CLASS, WE SHOW HOW CATEGORIES OF CLASS, RACE, GENDER, SEXUALITY AND DISABILITY ARE ENTANGLED.

WE HAVE TRIED TO ACKNOWLEDGE THE MATERIAL INEQUALITIES BETWEEN CLASS GROUPS, WHILE ALSO RECOGNIZING THE GOOD THINGS THAT COME FROM WORKING-CLASS EXPERIENCE.

ROADMAP

We've written this book so that it can be dipped in and out of – you don't need to read it cover to cover. The pages are grouped into these sections:

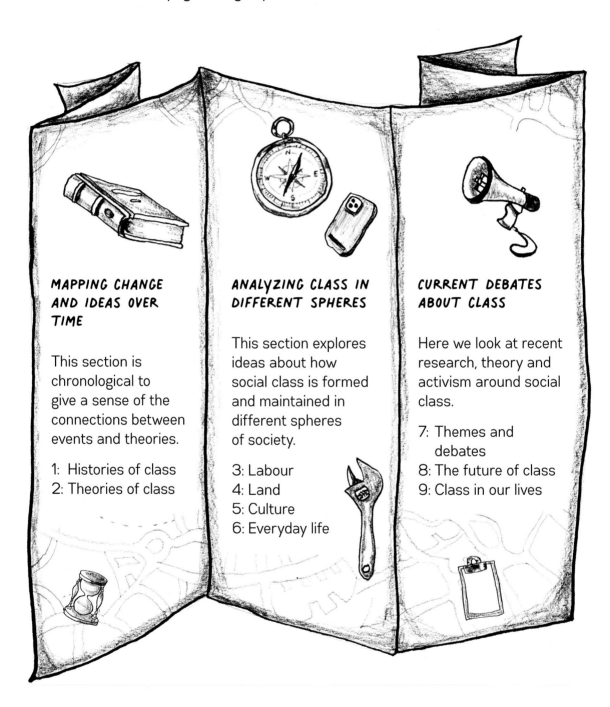

MAPPING CHANGE AND IDEAS OVER TIME

This section is chronological to give a sense of the connections between events and theories.

1: Histories of class
2: Theories of class

ANALYZING CLASS IN DIFFERENT SPHERES

This section explores ideas about how social class is formed and maintained in different spheres of society.

3: Labour
4: Land
5: Culture
6: Everyday life

CURRENT DEBATES ABOUT CLASS

Here we look at recent research, theory and activism around social class.

7: Themes and debates
8: The future of class
9: Class in our lives

We finish by encouraging you to think about social class in your own life and suggest different ways you can take action to challenge class inequalities.

CHAPTER 1: HISTORIES OF CLASS

Concepts are not neutral – they are created in specific historical and social moments as tools to describe and explain the world. Concepts can also have an impact on the world – in organizing social life, justifying how things are and pointing to strategies for change. In the next few pages, we will consider how the concept of class has been used and how it has travelled through time and space.

SOCIAL STRUCTURES

Early humans lived in small groups, hunting and gathering food to survive. The invention of agriculture, around 12,000 years ago, enabled the emergence of larger, more complex societies. Farming and the ability to store and transport surplus crops meant that not everyone had to be involved in the production of food. This created a division of labour within societies and the conditions for the accumulation of resources by some groups. As ancient cities emerged and communicated with each other via trade, complex social structures and hierarchies developed.

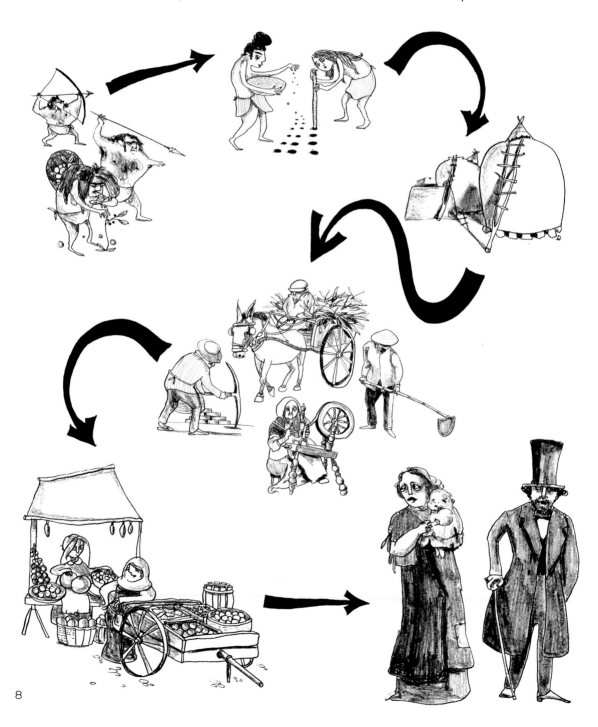

GLOBAL CONNECTIONS

The social structures that have developed in different local areas across the world are diverse but also connected through histories of migration, trade, imperialism, slavery, colonialism, rebellion and war. We often think of hierarchies and power inequalities as inevitable or natural, but by digging under the surface we can examine the social, economic and cultural factors that have had an impact on the way society is organized.

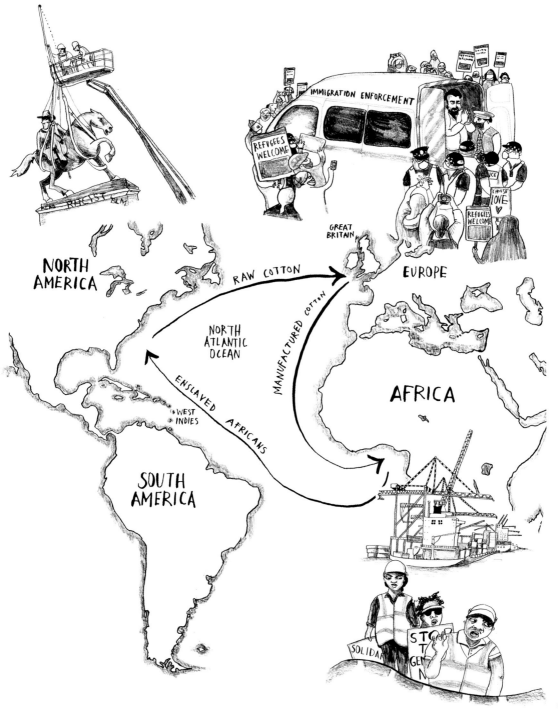

WHAT IS "CLASS"?

The word "class" is usually used to categorize people in relation to their economic position and social status. Depending on your perspective, these categories are used to describe and explain:

- economic and social inequality between groups
- the access that different groups have to resources (like land, property, power or money)
- a social hierarchy related to job type, education and family background.

Although there is considerable variation in the way that the term "class" is used in everyday language and by theorists, it is almost always used to make claims about inequality.

THE WAY THAT PEOPLE DESCRIBE PATTERNS OF INEQUALITY CONTAINS ASSUMPTIONS ABOUT WHY INEQUALITY EXISTS AND HOW REWARDS AND RESOURCES COME TO BE ALLOCATED IN AN UNEQUAL FASHION.

SOCIOLOGIST WENDY BOTTERO

THIS IS UNFAIR.

WHY? I'VE WORKED HARD TO GET HERE.

I WORK HARD TOO, AND MY JOB IS ESSENTIAL.

EXPLAINING INEQUALITY

> "CLASS" SUGGESTED A POTENTIAL FOR CHANGE, WHETHER BY CO-OPERATION, COMPETITION OR CONFLICT. IT REFERRED TO SOCIO-ECONOMIC POSITION, INTO WHICH AN INDIVIDUAL COULD RISE OR FALL, RATHER THAN TO STATUS PASSED ON BY BIRTH.

PENELOPE J. CORFIELD

Historian Penelope J. Corfield argues that class came into use as a concept in Britain in the 18th century. In earlier centuries, social status was relatively fixed and hereditary. With the emergence of capitalism, wealth and status could be gained via manufacture and trade. As the century progressed, increasing numbers of working people became reliant on wage labour instead of small-scale farming. Before this, there had been words to describe and explain social hierarchy, such as "ranks", "orders" or "stations", but the term "class" connected social position more explicitly to economics and production.

REBELLION

Across the world, the idea of social hierarchy as something changeable has developed against a backdrop of resistance and revolt against poverty and inequalities. Peasant uprisings, rebellions and revolutions against slavery, colonial rule, monarchy and capitalism have had an impact on social structure and the stories we tell about it.

In the Haitian Revolution of 1791–1804, enslaved Africans in the French colony of Saint-Domingue fought for freedom from colonialism and slavery. The revolution led to Haitian independence and the emancipation of slaves. This has been a source of inspiration for liberation movements, literature and anti-racist activism.

WE HAVE KNOWN HOW TO FACE DANGERS TO OBTAIN OUR LIBERTY, WE SHALL KNOW HOW TO BRAVE DEATH TO MAINTAIN IT.

TOUSSAINT LOUVERTURE, C.1743–1803. LEADER OF THE SUCCESSFUL HAITIAN REVOLUTION AGAINST EUROPEAN SLAVERY AND COLONIALISM.

DON'T BUY SEGREGATION

WE DEMAND EQUAL RIGHTS NOW!

WE MARCH FOR INTEGRATED SCHOOLS NOW!

NO JUSTICE NO PEACE

BLACK LIVES MATTER

GET YOUR KNEE OFF OUR NECKS

THE ENLIGHTENMENT

The 18th century saw the emergence of an intellectual movement in Europe that historians have called "the Enlightenment". Although there was diversity and debate among thinkers writing at that time, Enlightenment philosophers shared a belief that they were creating universal knowledge through science and reason.

NATURALIST AND ANTHROPOLOGIST JOHANN FRIEDRICH BLUMENBACH, 1752–1840

Enlightenment philosophers were writing in the context of the expansion of European colonialism and slavery. The drive to measure the natural and social worlds, which continued into the 19th century, included the classification of people by race, class and sex. These classifications were used to justify European violence and domination across the world. The idea of natural or hereditary differences was also used to explain continuing poverty and inequality within European countries.

Many Enlightenment thinkers put forward ideas of equality and freedom. However, some of the movement's most famous thinkers were actively involved in the administration of colonialism and invested in slavery.

The famous thinkers associated with this time, such as Kant, Voltaire, Rousseau and Locke, were writing in Europe, and Enlightenment thinking was influential in the development of "Western" philosophy. This was central to European claims of superiority; however, historians have shown that the Enlightenment was influenced by ideas from around the world, including Confucianism (a philosophy developed in ancient China).

SCIENTIFIC RACISM

Writer Kenan Malik argues that the biological ideas about race that became more widespread among European scientists in the 19th century were a response to the social conditions of the time. Capitalist and colonial expansion met with rebellion and resistance. Theories about "natural" differences seemed to offer a scientific justification for the persistence of hierarchies. Malik argues that mid-Victorian racial science was not just about place of birth or colour but also about social position.

SCIENTIFIC RACISM HELPED GENERATE A HIERARCHY THAT JUSTIFIED THE SUPERIORITY OF THE RULING CLASS AT HOME AND ABROAD. IT PROCLAIMED THE FITNESS OF THE CAPITALIST CLASS TO RULE OVER THE WORKING CLASS AND OF THE WHITE RACE TO RULE OVER THE BLACK. IT DID SO NOT IN THE NAME OF DIVINE WILL OR ARISTOCRATIC REACTION BUT OF SCIENCE AND PROGRESS.

KENAN MALIK

SLAVERY SHOULD BE OUTLAWED.

I'VE GOT SCIENCE ON MY SIDE — WE'RE THE MORE ADVANCED RACE.

THE MEASUREMENT OF SKULLS WAS RIDDLED WITH STATISTICAL PROBLEMS AND BIAS; SCIENTISTS WERE LED BY THEIR ASSUMPTIONS ABOUT RACIAL RANKING.

PALEONTOLOGIST STEPHEN JAY GOULD

EUGENICS

In Britain, industrial capitalism had created a new urban working class, whose lives and living conditions were subject to scrutiny and control, including from social reformers who sought to "improve" people in the "lower" or "dangerous" classes.

The eugenics movement originated in late 19th-century Britain with the work of scientist Francis Galton (1822–1911); it brought together classification of the natural and social worlds, linear ideas about evolution and progress, and arguments about hereditary differences. Eugenicists argued that many human traits, including behaviour, were inherited and argued for "selective breeding" to "improve" society. The movement spread globally throughout the 19th and 20th centuries.

These ideas have been used to justify violence at all levels of society, including the forced sterilization and detention of those deemed "unfit", colonial invasion, racialized chattel slavery and genocide.

Historian Douglas Baynton argues that in the United States at the turn of the 20th century, evolutionary theories of human progress and industrialization had a significant impact on attitudes and discrimination towards people with disabilities. This included segregation, institutionalization, prohibition of marriage and blocking people with disabilities from entering the USA as migrants.

AMERICANS FOUND THEMSELVES DRAWN INTO A COMPETITIVE ECONOMY IN WHICH EFFICIENCY WAS VALUED. EVOLUTIONARY CONCEPTS AND METAPHORS FROM BIOLOGY WERE BEING APPLIED TO SOCIAL QUESTIONS. PEOPLE WHO WERE UNABLE TO COMPETE IN THIS MARKET, WHETHER BECAUSE OF DISABILITY, DISCRIMINATION OR BOTH, BEGAN TO BE TREATED AS THREATS TO PROGRESS.

DOUGLAS BAYNTON

YOU'RE NOT FIT TO WORK, SO YOU'RE OF NO VALUE TO ME.

VALUE?

SURVIVAL OF THE FITTEST... IT'S THE NATURAL WAY OF THE WORLD.

CLASSIFYING SEX AND SEXUALITY

Since the 19th century, the drive to categorize the population has been influential across many fields of study, including sociology, psychology, sexology, anthropology and demography. At the same time as scientists were seeking to classify social class and race, these emerging fields also set out to categorize people by sex and sexuality.

Much of this work sought to pin down "essential" differences between people and to explain social hierarchies. In some cases, the work was used to justify existing inequalities, and in others it was motivated by a drive for social reform.

Some feminist scholars and activists have used the concept of "gender" to differentiate between *social* and *biological* aspects of these classifications. The sex/gender distinction itself has also been the subject of debate. Some academics, such as Judith Butler, have pointed to the social aspects of sex as a classification.

The 19th century in Europe saw continued debates about the causes of inequality and unease about the behaviour and health of people living in poverty. Historian Lynette Finch argues that the Enlightenment belief that everything is knowable through research led to social surveys that aimed to categorize the urban poor, making moral judgements about observable behaviour concerning alcohol, childcare and sexuality. This meant that women's behaviour in particular, and the family, came under close scrutiny.

Surveys tried to map the lives of people living in these worlds that were "unknown" to the middle-class researchers – whether in the urban slums of Europe or the European colonies.

DISGUSTING! THESE CHILDREN ARE RUNNING RIOT. WHERE ARE THEIR PARENTS? DRUNK, I ASSUME. THESE STREETS AREN'T SAFE TO WALK ON ALONE!

IN THE 1840S SOCIAL COMMENTATORS VOICED ALARM ABOUT A THREAT TO SOCIAL ORDER SIMMERING AT THE DOORSTEP OF POLITE, MIDDLE-CLASS SOCIETY. IN SOCIAL SURVEYS OF THE URBAN POOR, MIDDLE-CLASS OBSERVERS DIVIDED "THE WORKING CLASS" INTO THOSE THEY DEEMED "RESPECTABLE" AND THOSE WHO WERE NOT.

LYNETTE FINCH

MAPPING CLASS

A prominent social commentator, Charles Booth (1840–1916) worked with a group of researchers on an inquiry into poverty in London in the late 19th century. They produced colour-coded maps, created from observations by School Board visitors and researchers.

MAPS DESCRIPTIVE OF LONDON POVERTY

LOWEST CLASS. VICIOUS, SEMI-CRIMINAL

VERY POOR, CASUAL. CHRONIC WANT

POOR. 18s TO 20s A WEEK FOR A MODERATE FAMILY

MIXED. SOME COMFORTABLE OTHERS POOR

FAIRLY COMFORTABLE. GOOD ORDINARY EARNINGS

MIDDLE CLASS. WELL TO DO

UPPER-MIDDLE & UPPER CLASSES. WEALTHY.

SOCIOLOGIST MIKE SAVAGE

BOOTH'S RESEARCH CONFLATED CLASS WITH RESPECTABILITY AND MORALITY. IT WAS IN THIS CONTEXT OF CONCERNS ABOUT RESPECTABILITY, CONTAMINATION AND THE CLASS DIVIDE THAT THE FIRST FORMAL MEASURES OF CLASS WERE DEVELOPED BY THE REGISTRAR GENERAL'S OFFICE IN 1911 TO ORGANIZE HOUSEHOLDS INTO SOCIAL CLASSES.

MEASURING CLASS

The "measurement" of social class has been subject to ongoing debate among social scientists. Most official systems of classification have attempted to map and analyze inequalities in society connected to the division of labour. Some of these, such as the Registrar General Schema, which Mike Savage talked about on the previous page, map out a hierarchy of occupations. Others have developed classifications based on different types of occupations and their relationships with each other (like the difference between people employing others, working for a salary or being paid by the hour).

THE ORIGINS OF CLASS CLASSIFICATION CANNOT BE REMOVED FROM AN ELITIST CONCERN TO DEMARCATE AND MAP THE BOUNDARY OF RESPECTABILITY BETWEEN MIDDLE (NON-MANUAL) AND WORKING (MANUAL) CLASSES.

MIKE SAVAGE

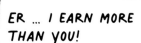

ER ... I EARN MORE THAN YOU!

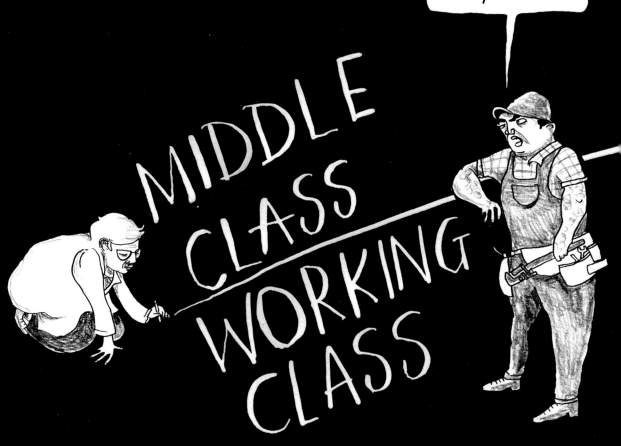

CREATING KNOWLEDGE ABOUT CLASS

Enlightenment ideas about reason and what counts as "legitimate" knowledge have had a profound impact. Philosopher Enrique Dussel argues that, through military and colonial violence and domination, Europeans extracted resources and information from cultures around the world, presenting the philosophy developed in the process as "universal". This has denied and excluded other forms of knowledge about social life, such as those created by indigenous, colonized and oppressed communities.

MOVE OUT OF THE WAY. YOU'RE PREVENTING PROGRESS!

WE ARE ALL CONNECTED WITH THE LAND AND WATER — THIS ISN'T SOMETHING ONE PERSON CAN "OWN".

ALL OF THE WORLD'S GREAT CULTURES HAVE CREATED PHILOSOPHIES. EUROPEAN PHILOSOPHY WAS REGIONAL, BUT FROM THE 16TH CENTURY BEGAN TO PRESENT ITSELF AS UNIVERSAL. WE NEED DIALOGUE AND EDUCATION ABOUT MULTIPLE PHILOSOPHICAL TRADITIONS.

ENRIQUE DUSSEL

CASTE AND CLASS

Systems of stratification and social hierarchy are a product of the histories and social relations in different times and places.

For example, historian Romila Thapar argues that ideas about "caste" as an inherited social hierarchy have existed in India for 2,000 years. The idea of caste combines different systems of stratification, including divisions between different occupations. Thapar shows that, although caste is often presented as an unchanging structure, there have been variations in the way that it has worked in different regions and time periods.

Sociologist Vinay Bahl argues that, in India, caste and class have entangled histories. These systems of social hierarchy have shifted through changing forms of production, land ownership and use, religion, British colonialism and the rise of capitalist production.

THE BRITISH FOUND IN THE "CASTE SYSTEM" A USEFUL STRUCTURE ON WHICH THEY COULD BUILD A STRONG ECONOMIC AND SOCIAL BASE IN INDIA FOR THEMSELVES.

VINAY BAHL

GLOBAL CLASSES

The intensification of globalization has had an impact on the way that social class operates across borders. Although the movement of people is often tightly restricted and violently policed, the rise of transnational, global corporations has meant that money and goods link classes together worldwide through the production, trade and consumption of goods.

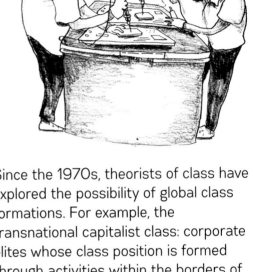

Since the 1970s, theorists of class have explored the possibility of global class formations. For example, the transnational capitalist class: corporate elites whose class position is formed through activities within the borders of the nation and in the international sphere.

THE EXTRAORDINARY CONCENTRATION OF ECONOMIC POWER IN TRANSNATIONAL CORPORATIONS EXERTS A HUGE AMOUNT OF POWER SOCIALLY, CULTURALLY AND POLITICALLY ACROSS THE WORLD.

SOCIOLOGIST WILLIAM I. ROBINSON

CHAPTER 2: THEORIES OF CLASS

We will explore the ideas of many theorists throughout the book, introducing you to a range of explanations for the emergence and persistence of class inequality. In this chapter, we'll look at thinkers influential in the academic study of social class. Some of the first thinkers we will meet are often described as "foundational" for the development of sociology – the study of society.

Ideas are powerful and have real world consequences; some have informed how economies are structured, governments are run and social movements are organized.

For example, Marxism remains the ideology of several communist states and the ruling parties of China, Cuba, Laos and Vietnam. Spivak's post-colonial critique influences education in the poorest regions of the world, where teaching can empower local communities, and in global higher education by making literature of the global South fundamental rather than marginal. In the USA, W.E.B. Du Bois founded *The Crisis*, the official magazine for the National Association for the Advancement of Colored People, which aimed to show the danger of racial prejudice and social injustice in the USA.

MARXISM AND THE CLASS DIVIDE

The iconic philosopher Karl Marx (1818–83) argued that in a capitalist society, people are divided into economic categories based on their role in production. **Capitalism** is an economic and political system where the production of goods and their trade is controlled by private owners for profit, rather than by the state. In Marx's view, there are two classes under capitalism:

- the proletariat: the working class who earn a wage by producing the things used in society
- the bourgeoisie: the capitalist class who own the "means of production" – the resources and tools needed to produce the things that meet human needs.

Marx's ideas about social class were developed through an approach he called "historical materialism". He argued, along with Friedrich Engels, that society could be understood by analyzing how human beings worked to meet their **material needs**, such as for food and shelter. They argued that these economic processes of production are what create **social relations** – such as the inequality between the bourgeoisie and proletariat.

DURKHEIM

Émile Durkheim (1858–1917), like Marx, was trying to understand the changes occuring in society during his lifetime. They both lived through the processes of **industrialization** and **urbanization** that defined the shift from traditional to modern society. However, they took very different approaches to understanding society.

Marx thought modern society was being forged through class conflict - the exploitation of the working class by the capitalist class. But Durkheim saw a society that continued to function, and he was interested in how social and moral solidarity were maintained.

Durkheim argued that the industrial changes producing new divisions of labour led to the emergence of new forms of solidarity.

Traditional society: Mechanical solidarity

- In societies where most people have similar roles, they are bound together by their shared experience. This forms a strong consensus, where values and beliefs are shared.

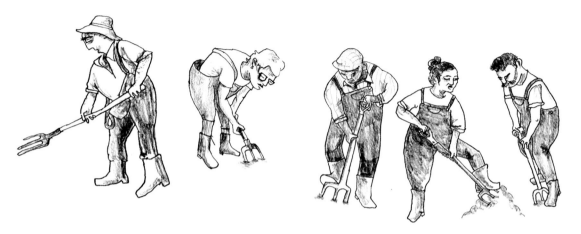

Modern society: Organic solidarity

- Industrialization led to an increased diversification of roles, meaning that people were no longer connected by shared experience. Rather, solidarity in modern societies is based on economic interdependence.

ORGANIC SOLIDARITY GROWS OUT OF THE DIVISION OF LABOUR, BUT ONLY WHEN THIS IS SPONTANEOUS. CLASS CONFLICT CAN DISRUPT SOLIDARITY, BUT IT IS A SYMPTOM OF SOCIAL PROBLEMS NOT ITS CAUSE.

ÉMILE DURKHEIM

DU BOIS

W.E.B. Du Bois (1868–1963) was a groundbreaking scholar who combined historical analysis with empirical research, such as interviews, surveys, maps and observation, to analyze the social position and experiences of African Americans. Du Bois argued that detailed scientific investigation was needed to understand society – that our analysis should come from observation, rather than the abstract theorizing that was dominant in early American sociology and which Du Bois called "car window sociology".

THE PROBLEM WITH THE BLACK FOLKS IN THE SOUTH IS THAT THEY ARE LAZY.

CAR-WINDOW SOCIOLOGISTS DON'T SEE THAT HE HAS BEEN UP SINCE DAWN, PAYS HUGE RENTS TO THE WHITE LANDOWNER, AND WORKS HARD WHEN HE NEEDS TO. HE DOESN'T SEE WHY HE SHOULD SAVE THE LANDOWNER'S CORN.

W.E.B. DU BOIS

His work challenged scientific racism and biological accounts of racial inequality, foregrounding the role of social, economic and cultural factors and exploring the relationship between race, class and gender. His pioneering empirical work was marginalized by White-dominated sociology of the time.

THE COLOR LINE AND MAPPING AFRICAN AMERICAN LIVES

Du Bois argued that racial oppression and segregation were woven into the development of capitalism through colonialism and slavery. Du Bois' work examined both the historical roots of White supremacy and its continued impact in the lives of African Americans. Du Bois argued that racial difference has been used by White people to justify denying resources and rights to people of colour across the world.

> THE PROBLEM OF THE 20TH CENTURY IS THE PROBLEM OF THE COLOR LINE — THE RELATION OF THE DARKER TO THE LIGHTER RACES OF MEN IN ASIA AND AFRICA, IN AMERICA AND THE ISLANDS OF THE SEA.

W.E.B. DU BOIS

Du Bois' analysis of African Americans living in Philadelphia highlighted shared experiences of racial oppression, but also explored class divisions among African Americans. Du Bois produced a statistical analysis of Black families, categorizing them into grades in relation to their employment and income. He combined this with observations and descriptions of the everyday lives of the people in each of these classes, from their work and housing to their social lives and entertainment.

WEBER

Sociologist Max Weber (1864–1920) believed society to be characterized by conflicts over power and resources. He argued that our social position is defined by the interconnection between class, status and "party".

Class: Although Weber agreed with Marx that class is based on objective economic conditions (the unequal distribution of material resources), he thought there were important economic factors beyond property ownership. He pointed to the different conditions experienced by workers, suggesting that their skills and qualifications shaped what type of job they were able to get – what he called their "market position". Acquiring marketable resources enabled workers to achieve better working conditions and higher wages.

Weber defined class in terms of:

• the ownership of property
• the possession of skills that can be sold.

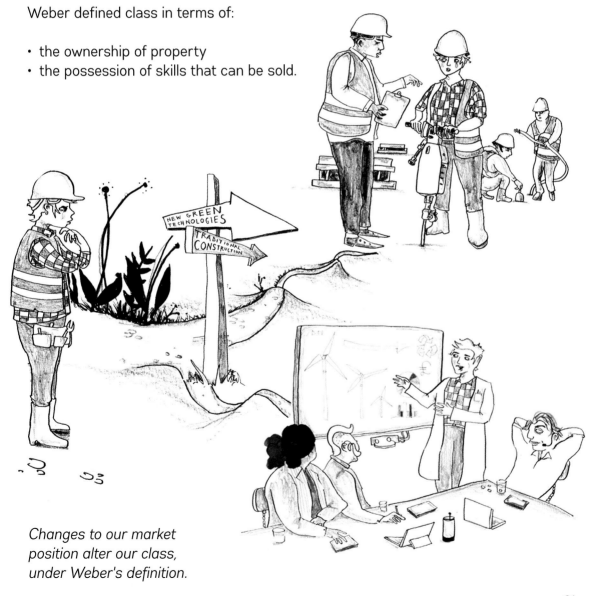

Changes to our market position alter our class, under Weber's definition.

Status: According to Weber, our social standing is communicated through our lifestyles. We are able to recognize others with a shared identity and status through their dress, how they talk and where they live. Although high wealth often implies a high status, they can vary independently.

DIFFERENCES IN THE STYLES OF BEARD AND HAIRDO, CLOTHES, FOOD AND EATING HABITS, AND ALL KINDS OF OTHER VISIBLE DIFFERENCES CAN GIVE RISE TO REPULSION AND CONTEMPT.

MAX WEBER

I'M SORRY, THIS IS A BLACK TIE EVENT.

DON'T YOU KNOW WHO I AM?! I WROTE THE PLAY!

SHAME PUDDING

THE NOBLE THEATRE

Party: Weber was interested in how individuals gain power through collective action. Party refers to a group of individuals working together towards a common goal. They include political parties, trade unions, groups who aim to tackle a specific problem and recreational groups such as sports clubs. Party membership is often based on shared backgrounds and beliefs and can cut across class lines.

HOMES FOR WILD LIFE NOT PEOPLE

SAVE **OUR** WOODS

PETITION

GREEN SPACES FOR ALL

GRAMSCI

Philosopher Antonio Gramsci (1891–1937) famously wrote his essays on political theory while he was imprisoned in Italy by Mussolini's fascist regime. He developed Marx's idea that the economic base of society is legitimized by ideological superstructures such as education and religion. An **ideology** is a system of ideas or ideals which form the basis of political systems and organizations.

Gramsci called the dominant beliefs produced by these superstructures "**hegemony**". He argued that hegemony is a system of domination that rules not through force or coercion but through consent. The ruling classes achieve domination by establishing "common sense". We all look to "common sense" to guide our everyday actions, which means we do not question inequality and exploitation.

33

ALTHUSSER

Louis Althusser (1918-90) was a structuralist Marxist who, like Gramsci, wanted to understand how capitalism is reproduced. Rejecting economic determinism (the Marxist idea that all of society is based on economic relationships), they both looked beyond workplace production to the role of ideas in reproducing capitalist systems. Althusser wanted to explain why workers were unable to free themselves from capitalist exploitation. Building upon Gramsci's ideological superstructures, Althusser argued that ideology is reproduced through institutional systems – what he called apparatuses.

Repressive state apparatuses maintain rule through force. They are the arms of the state, such as the police and army, that support capitalist class structure by repressing any threats to those structures.

Ideological state apparatuses operate less by force and more through ideology. They encourage people to imagine their place within society by imposing systems of thought through education, religion and the family.

These state apparatuses produce the ideologies through which our own thoughts and feelings are constituted, a process Althusser called "interpellation". This means that our behaviour is defined by the rituals and practices of the state apparatuses rather than by our own individual agency.

There are ongoing debates about whether Althusser's work should be taught. On the one hand, his ideas have informed contemporary theories of class and therefore should be referenced. On the other, separating his thoughts from his actions ignores the violence he committed against Hélène Rytmann and further entrenches the harms of gender-based violence today.

WHEN WE WERE WRITING THIS BOOK, WE FOUND OUT THAT ALTHUSSER MURDERED THE SOCIOLOGIST HÉLÈNE RYTMANN, WHO WAS HIS WIFE. WE TALKED ABOUT WHETHER WE SHOULD REMOVE HIM FROM THE BOOK.

ALTHUSSER'S IDEAS HAVE BEEN VERY INFLUENTIAL IN THEORIES ABOUT SOCIAL CLASS. NEITHER OF US HAD HEARD ABOUT THE MURDER, DESPITE HAVING READ AND BEEN TAUGHT ABOUT ALTHUSSER, SO WE DECIDED TO OUTLINE HIS IDEAS BUT ALSO TALK ABOUT THE ISSUES WITH THIS.

RANCIÈRE

The philosopher Jacques Rancière is critical of Althusser's perspective, which he believes creates a distinction between the knowledgeable academic and the unknowing working class. For Rancière the fundamental feature of domination is the refusal to see, hear or recognize the voices of the oppressed.

Rancière argues that classic Marxism plays a role in this type of domination by assuming workers don't understand their own exploitation (what Marxists call "false class consciousness"). Instead, he shifts our attention to how the accepted order of things is created and maintained. He calls this order the "**distribution of the sensible**".

The distribution of the sensible refers both to what a community shares – which identities it recognizes and who it deems worth listening to – and to the divisions within a community which define who has a claim to what.

The Jim Crow Laws mandated the racial segregation of public facilities in the Southern United States. They were enforced from the 1870s until 1965.

Rancière argues that the distribution of the sensible can be ruptured and transformed by acts of politics. When people who are excluded demand recognition, the distribution of the sensible is transformed through **dissensus**.

Sit-in acts of civil disobedience during the US civil rights movement.

FANON

Frantz Fanon (1925–61) was a philosopher and psychiatrist whose work explored the impacts of anti-Black racism, the violence of colonialism and decolonial revolution. He was born in the French colony of Martinique, studied psychiatry in France and led a ward in a psychiatric hospital in Algeria.

Fanon argued that colonialism dehumanizes people whose lands and cultures have been colonized. He theorized class in relation to race as grounded in economic exploitation, but he also explored the psychological dimensions of this, particularly for people living under colonialism. He argued that racism enables the capitalist class to divide workers.

According to Fanon there were four different classes in decolonial struggle: peasants; the lumpenproletariat; the proletariat; and bourgeoisie.

THE PEASANT, THE DECLASSED PERSON, THE STARVING PERSON, IS THE EXPLOITED PERSON WHO DISCOVERS SOONEST THAT VIOLENCE ALONE PAYS. FOR HIM, THERE IS NO COMPROMISE, NO POSSIBILITY OF COMING TO TERMS.

FRANTZ FANON

The Lumpenproletariat
- Not in regular paid work
- Most likely to join the peasants in revolutionary action

The Proletariat
- Employed in work that supports the functioning of colonialism
- Has a greater stake in the survival of colonialism and neocolonialism, so less likely to engage in revolution

Bourgeoisie
- Emerges at the end of colonial rule
- Unable to accumulate capital; relies on a relationship with the colonial power

One of the most influential aspects of Fanon's work was his analysis of the psychological and embodied aspects of colonialism and racism. His work brought together clinical analysis with an investigation of the economic and social conditions of colonialism.

Fanon argued that colonial ideas about racial superiority and inferiority shape relationships between White and Black people, and that these ideas become powerfully internalized.

BOURDIEU

Sociologist Pierre Bourdieu (1930-2002) argued that class is not only an economic position but also social and cultural. His theory of class brings together structure and agency in order to understand the reproduction of class and social change. He argued that we need a theory of class which connects the hierarchies of society with individual experiences.

Structure: Structures are factors which are external to the individual yet determine their action - for example, religion, the state, economics and class. So, a structure is something that makes us who we are; it shapes our possibilities and, some would argue, determines our desires, so that we want what our structured position allows.

Agency: Agency can be thought of as the characteristics of the individual which serve to construct the world around them. So, agency refers to the ways in which we are able to make choices, negotiate, act and interact.

BOURDIEU'S THEORETICAL TOOL KIT

"**Habitus**" refers to the connection between our personal experiences and our position in the social world. It's made up of our dispositions: how we walk, talk and the way we think. Although habitus refers to subjective experience, it's not purely individual: other people from a similar background will share these dispositions. The differences in behaviour we can see between classes are a product of unequal access to resources.

Bourdieu calls these resources "**capital**". He argues that the distribution of capitals represents the structure of the social world. For Bourdieu, there are three forms of capital:

- Economic: Money and property
- Social: Friendships and networks
- Cultural: Understanding and appreciation of good taste

Bourdieu visualizes society as made up of various "**fields**". We enter fields with different amounts of accumulated capitals embodied in our habitus, and this informs our relative position within the field. Those with capitals that are valued within the field enter with a "feel for the game" and are able to achieve a dominant position.

WHEN OUR HABITUS MATCHES THE DOMINANT VALUES OF THE FIELD AND WE HAVE THE RIGHT FORMS OF CAPITAL, WE CAN MOVE THROUGH THE SOCIAL WORLD UNINHIBITED AND MAY NOT NOTICE THE BARRIERS OTHERS FACE.

PIERRE BOURDIEU

KEEP UP!

GIDDENS

Sociologist Anthony Giddens developed the concept "**structuration**" in order to explain the active process of making and remaking social structures. He believes structure and action are connected – we only have structures because people act in predictable ways, and we can only act because we have access to structures of knowledge. Giddens calls this connection the "duality of structure". Social structures such as education, the criminal justice system and the family only exist because individuals constantly make them through their everyday practice.

SPIVAK

Drawing upon Gramsci's definition of the **subaltern** as those excluded and displaced from the socio-economic institutions of society, Gayatri Chakravorty Spivak questions the use of subaltern studies in post-colonial India. She is critical of Western intellectuals who try to write about and understand the subaltern from the outside. By transforming indigenous knowledge into "data" and the intellectual property of the author, the subaltern are homogenized and ascribed an identity that excludes agency and assumes they cannot speak for themselves.

Spivak explores the historical and ideological factors that obstruct this possibility of being heard. As a post-modern feminist thinker, she argues that human consciousness is constructed through the language we have access to. Therefore, subalternity is a position without identity, because there is no recognized framework to speak of subaltern agency and resistance.

WHEN I SAY THE SUBALTERN CANNOT SPEAK, IT MEANS THAT IF SPEAKING INVOLVES SPEAKING AND LISTENING, THIS POSSIBILITY OF RESPONSE, RESPONSIBILITY, DOES NOT EXIST IN THE SUBALTERN'S SPHERE.

CAN THE SUBALTERN SPEAK?

> FOR SO LONG EVERYONE HAS WANTED TO HOLD ON TO THE BELIEF THAT THE UNITED STATES IS A CLASS-FREE SOCIETY — THAT ANYONE WHO WORKS HARD ENOUGH CAN MAKE IT TO THE TOP. FEW PEOPLE STOP TO THINK THAT IN A CLASS-FREE SOCIETY THERE WOULD BE NO TOP.

bell hooks

bell hooks (1952–2021) was a Black feminist thinker who suggested that we must explore the interlocking nature of race, gender and class. She drew upon her own experience of moving from a working-class background to a world of affluence to argue that we need to raise class consciousness in order to know how to struggle against economic inequality.

hooks explained that the feminist movement emphasizes values of caring and sharing in opposition to capitalist commodifictation. She argued that reducing our value to that of our material possessions is dehumanizing. Both the poor and the wealthy need to give up their attachment to property to allow non-market values to thrive.

LACLAU & MOUFFE

Ernesto Laclau and Chantal Mouffe's book *Hegemony and Socialist Strategy* (1985) was central in the development of post-Marxist thought (the development and re-thinking of classic Marxism from the 1970s). They questioned the inconsistencies in Gramsci's work, asking why we should analyse the role of dominant ideas, if class is determined by economics.

Taking a post-structural approach (exploring the processes through which class is *made*, rather than *determined*), Laclau and Mouffe rejected the Marxist idea that society is shaped by underlying principles. For them, hegemony is not predetermined, and therefore new hegemonic discourses can be developed in order to achieve social change.

Laclau and Mouffe offered strategies for social movements to mobilize and generate change.

1. Social change is not deterministic.

Laclau and Mouffe challenged Marx's belief that revolution is an inevitable consequence of capitalism. There is nothing natural about the struggles against power and we therefore need to understand when, why and how certain social movements emerge and succeed.

2. Social change can involve a range of different social actors.

The increased complexity of modern society means that an antagonism based solely on class will not mobilize enough citizens to achieve social change.

3. Social change requires a discourse to help frame inequality as oppression.

The construction of social antagonism has become the key problem for those seeking social change. They must create a story that can mobilize multiple groups for the same cause. The story must connect inequality to injustice by drawing upon ideas that are already accepted in society.

Is it okay to convince someone they are in a relationship of oppression?

NEOLIBERALISM

> NEOLIBERAL IDEAS HAVE BEEN USED TO JUSTIFY POLITICAL INTERVENTIONS BY THE STATE WHICH ENABLE ECONOMIC ELITES TO MAINTAIN THEIR POWER.

DAVID HARVEY

Neoliberalism is an economic theory which suggests that society can be advanced through the extension of individual freedom and choice. State interventions should be kept minimal because the **market** drives the economy. The state's role is to secure and defend the market through property rights, free market and free trade. If markets do not exist, they must be created by the state, for example, in areas such as education and transport.

Neoliberalism involves the rollback of the state, reductions in public expenditure and the formation of "markets" within the public sector. This requires the transformation of the social contract between the state and the citizen, whereby citizens must negotiate access to services through the enactment of individual choice. Therefore, the citizen becomes responsible for their own safety and welfare, while the state facilitates the provision of services via a free market economy. The construction of the consumer-citizen reinforces inequality, as citizens who have greater resources to make choices accumulate wealth and are able to access the markets of service provision.

One of the central paradoxes of neoliberalism is that market failure often produces regimes of **austerity**, which further entrench neoliberal ideas. Austerity policies across different states share common features of neoliberal governance: reducing expenditure while not raising tax revenue; retrenchment in public services; and focusing budget cuts in areas that impact poor and marginalized populations. Austerity policies are legitimized through neoliberal ideas which redefine inequality as an individual problem.

SKEGGS

Beverley Skeggs is a feminist sociologist who argues that we need to shift our attention away from mapping classificatory systems to ask how and why classifications have been established. She recognizes systems of exchange beyond the economic, suggesting that class is marked onto our bodies by cultural and moral symbolic systems.

Skeggs explores the ways in which economic value and cultural values are entwined. In arguing this, she builds on the idea of "cultural capital" put forward by Bourdieu. However, she is critical of the assumption that economic value simply drives cultural values. She argues that those excluded from economic value express cultural values beyond capitalist logic. In doing so, her ideas help us to explore how different kinds of cultural capital circulate in different social contexts.

WE, THEREFORE, AS SOCIOLOGISTS, HAVE A DUTY TO LOOK BEYOND AND SEARCH FOR THE GAPS, THE UN-CAPTURED AND BETTER WAYS OF BEING AND DOING.

BEVERLEY SKEGGS

THIS SHOULD FIT YOUR LITTLE ONE NOW.

FORMULATING CLASS

As we have seen, there are lots of different and conflicting theoretical perspectives about social class. Not only do theorists disagree with each other about the foundations, formation and operation of class, but they also aren't always even talking about the same thing.

One thing that writers agree on is that class is something social. Theorists explore how it is produced through different social spheres, such as the organization of labour, the distribution of land, the production of culture and everyday life. In the next four chapters, we will look at ideas about how class is made in these different spheres.

CHAPTER 3: LABOUR

Many theories of class start from the idea that our position in society is connected to the work or labour that we do. The "classical" theorists of class each had slightly different perspectives on this relationship between labour and class.

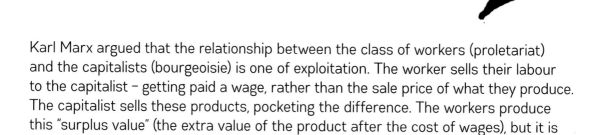

Karl Marx argued that the relationship between the class of workers (proletariat) and the capitalists (bourgeoisie) is one of exploitation. The worker sells their labour to the capitalist – getting paid a wage, rather than the sale price of what they produce. The capitalist sells these products, pocketing the difference. The workers produce this "surplus value" (the extra value of the product after the cost of wages), but it is the capitalist who accumulates all the money. The capitalist is therefore in a position of dominance over the worker, who depends on their wages to survive.

This **materialist*** approach to social class says that our position in society is determined by where we sit in economic relations of production – who has to sell their labour to live? Who has ownership and control over the resources and tools needed to sustain human life?

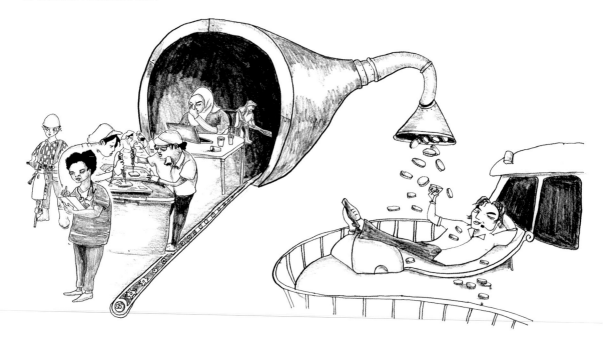

*Read page 26 for more on classical theorists and historical materialism.

Although the words "work" and "labour" are often used interchangeably, they can mean different things within different theoretical perspectives. In Marxist writing, the terms are used to differentiate between productive human activity in general ("work") and activity involved in the creation of value in capitalism ("labour"). There is some debate about what gets included in these categories. Sociologist Olivier Frayssé argues that the words used to explain different activities developed through historical and social relationships – for example, some of these words developed via references to pain, struggle, slavery, service and domination.

How we define work and labour is important to our understanding of class, including who we think is included in each class. For example, socialist feminists have argued that unpaid domestic labour is part of economic production, so those doing it are part of the working class. (We'll look at these ideas more closely on page 58.)

LABOUR IS AN ALIENATED FORM OF WORK, RELATED TO THE ORGANIZATION OF CLASSED SOCIETIES. WORK IS COMMON TO ALL SOCIETIES AND INVOLVES MAKING GOODS AND PROVIDING SERVICES THAT SATISFY HUMAN NEEDS.

SOCIOLOGISTS CHRISTIAN FUCHS & SEBASTIAN SEVIGNANI

WORK

LABOUR

COLONIALISM AND CLASS

The global nature of capitalism and its foundations in colonialism and slavery have shaped class inequalities within and between countries. European empires enslaved and exploited people and resources from colonized countries to build the wealth of their own nations. Scholar Shreeram Krishnaswami argues that this plunder played a key role in Western European capitalist expansion and global class formation. We see this process reflected now in the exploitation of migrant workers and the use of global outsourcing to cut the cost of labour and increase profits for corporations. Over the next few pages we'll look at how these colonial legacies continue to shape inequalities of gender, class and race.

THE INTENSIVE EXPLOITATION OF PEOPLE AND RESOURCES IN COLONIZED COUNTRIES MEANT THAT CAPITALISTS DID NOT ALWAYS HAVE TO INCREASE THE LEVEL OF EXPLOITATION OF WORKERS IN THEIR HOME COUNTRIES. THIS HELPED TO REDUCE THE LIKELIHOOD OF INDUSTRIAL STRUGGLES IN WESTERN EUROPE FROM BECOMING REVOLUTIONS.

SHREERAM KRISHNASWAMI

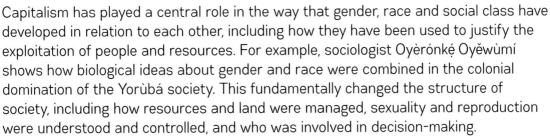

THE FUNDAMENTAL CATEGORY "WOMAN" SIMPLY DID NOT EXIST IN YORÙBÁLAND PRIOR TO ITS SUSTAINED CONTACT WITH THE WEST. FOR FEMALES, COLONIZATION IMPOSED A HIERARCHY IN WHICH THEY WERE CATEGORIZED AND OPPRESSED BY RACE AND GENDER.

OYÈRÓNKÉ OYĚWÙMÍ

Capitalism has played a central role in the way that gender, race and social class have developed in relation to each other, including how they have been used to justify the exploitation of people and resources. For example, sociologist Oyèrónké Oyěwùmí shows how biological ideas about gender and race were combined in the colonial domination of the Yorùbá society. This fundamentally changed the structure of society, including how resources and land were managed, sexuality and reproduction were understood and controlled, and who was involved in decision-making.

THEY CANNOT BE LEADERS BECAUSE THEY ARE WOMEN.

WE HAVE ALWAYS BEEN INVOLVED IN POLITICS AS CHIEFS AND OFFICIALS!

The relationship between colonialism, slavery, capitalism and class ties together working-class people across the world. A person making a sports shoe in a factory in Pakistan is connected with transport and delivery workers carrying it across borders to warehouses and consumers in the UK. The adverts that tell us our lives will be better if we buy things leave out the story about how those products were created.

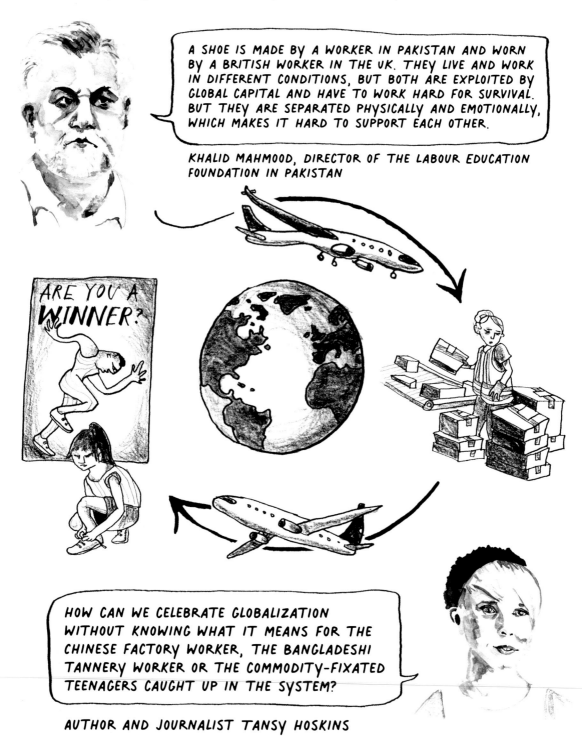

A SHOE IS MADE BY A WORKER IN PAKISTAN AND WORN BY A BRITISH WORKER IN THE UK. THEY LIVE AND WORK IN DIFFERENT CONDITIONS, BUT BOTH ARE EXPLOITED BY GLOBAL CAPITAL AND HAVE TO WORK HARD FOR SURVIVAL. BUT THEY ARE SEPARATED PHYSICALLY AND EMOTIONALLY, WHICH MAKES IT HARD TO SUPPORT EACH OTHER.

KHALID MAHMOOD, DIRECTOR OF THE LABOUR EDUCATION FOUNDATION IN PAKISTAN

ARE YOU A WINNER?

HOW CAN WE CELEBRATE GLOBALIZATION WITHOUT KNOWING WHAT IT MEANS FOR THE CHINESE FACTORY WORKER, THE BANGLADESHI TANNERY WORKER OR THE COMMODITY-FIXATED TEENAGERS CAUGHT UP IN THE SYSTEM?

AUTHOR AND JOURNALIST TANSY HOSKINS

MIGRATION

Social class has an impact on the movement of people from one place to another. The resources that people have access to affect patterns of migration – whether in search of work, safety or a different life. Migration connects up different class systems globally, and classes are shaped by histories of migration. The violent policing of borders, including the detention and deportation of people, is intimately tied to social class.

Immigration processes often divide people into those who are seen as "legitimate" and those who are "illegal". This has material impacts on who can access particular services (such as healthcare or domestic violence support) and categorizes particular groups of migrants as "other".

AUTHOR, ACTIVIST AND POET AKALA

Migration has an impact on social class position. Racialized hierarchies can mean that someone with relatively high status in one country can't always bring that class position with them when they migrate.

Migration also shapes class structure across borders. For example, money sent home from the global north plays a role in the formation of middle classes in the global south.

MIGRATION SHOWS THAT SOCIAL CLASS IS NOT A STABLE IDENTITY, BUT IS RELATIONAL. MIGRANTS USUALLY HAVE MULTIPLE CLASS STATUSES ACROSS THEIR LIFETIME AND IN DIFFERENT PLACES.

ANTHROPOLOGISTS CATI COE & JULIA PAULI

In the UK, systems of classification that categorize households in relation to paid employment emerged from the early 20th century onwards. Today, the UK Office of National Statistics (ONS) uses the National Statistics Socio-Economic Classification (NS-SEC)*. These systems try to explain the relationship between people's social and economic position in society and their behaviour, experiences and opportunities.

THESE CLASSIFICATION SYSTEMS ARE BASED ON THE IDEA THAT CLASSES HAVE DIFFERENT LIFE CHANCES.

WENDY BOTTERO

1.1 LARGE EMPLOYERS & HIGHER MANAGERIAL & ADMIN OCCUPATIONS

1.2 HIGHER PROFESSIONAL OCCUPATIONS

2. LOWER MANAGERIAL, ADMIN AND PROFESSIONAL OCCUPATIONS

3. INTERMEDIATE OCCUPATIONS

4. SELF-EMPLOYERS AND OWN ACCOUNT WORKERS

5. LOWER SUPERVISORY AND TECHNICAL OCCUPATIONS

6. SEMI-ROUTINE OCCUPATIONS

7. ROUTINE OCCUPATIONS

8. NEVER WORKED AND LONG-TERM UNEMPLOYED

NOT CLASSIFIED: STUDENTS, OCCUPATIONS NOT STATED OR INADEQUATELY DESCRIBED

NOT CLASSIFIABLE FOR OTHER REASONS

*Look at pages 20–21 for more detailed information on the emergence of these schemas.

CHANGES TO WORK

As the way that work is organized changes over time, the theories and categories we use to make sense of it change too. The measurement and classification of class often involves a distinction between manual and non-manual work, as we've seen. However, global shifts in industrial production and the rise in precarious, low-paid service work have blurred the distinctions between classes and different kinds of work.

WE NO LONGER HAVE A COUNTRY FULL OF FACTORIES, MINES AND MILLS WITH RIGID STRUCTURES OF WORKERS AND BOSSES. I GREW UP IN A GENERATION DEFINED BY WATCHING PEOPLE OLDER THAN ME BENEFIT FROM SEEMINGLY ENDLESS CREDIT, SO THE DEMARCATION BETWEEN RICH AND POOR WAS HARD TO SPOT. BY THE TIME I WAS 12, THE THEN PRIME MINISTER TONY BLAIR ANNOUNCED THAT HE WANTED TO SEE 50% OF YOUNG ADULTS IN HIGHER EDUCATION BY THE YEAR 2010. GOING TO UNIVERSITY WAS NO LONGER A CLEAR INDICATION OF CLASS. IN MY GENERATION, YOUR FIRST JOB WAS LIKELY TO BE ON A SHOP FLOOR, IN CATERING, OR IN A CALL CENTRE. POST-2008 RECESSION, THESE CATEGORIES HAVE BECOME EVEN MORE BLURRED AS JOB SECURITY FOR MOST BECAME A DREAM RATHER THAN A REALITY.

JOURNALIST AND AUTHOR RENI EDDO-LODGE

In places where heavy industry is at the centre of working-class community, the closure of factories is felt beyond the loss of jobs. Psychologists Valerie Walkerdine and Luis Jimenez have explored the role of iron and steel production in Wales, and the losses and trauma experienced across generations as a result.

In the town in South Wales in which they carried out their research, men who might have traditionally worked in steel production were faced with unemployment, or taking up service-sector jobs, which were often seen as "feminine". They explore how this impacted the gendered dynamics within communities and families, including the shaming of men working in jobs like cleaning and retail. They also argue that traumatic experiences of unemployment, shame and despair over decades can be transmitted through generations, as each tries to cope with the loss of jobs in the community.

UNPAID LABOUR AND SOCIAL REPRODUCTION

Feminists have argued that unpaid labour, particularly care and domestic work such as childcare, cooking, cleaning and caring for friends and relatives, should be included in our analysis of class in capitalism. This work is disproportionately done by women and people of colour.

In 2017, Afroza Anwary interviewed managers, supervisors and workers in FB Fashion, a garment factory in Bangladesh. The majority of the workers in the factory are women, working long hours for low pay, and often required to work overtime for free. In addition to the factory work, the women are responsible for childcare and housework. She argues that all of this work – paid and unpaid, in the home and in the factory – is part of a global chain of commodity production. Clothing companies profit by paying less than the value of the products the workers make. The workers are afraid to lose their jobs, so the companies can impose unreasonable working conditions and demand free labour. The women's work in the home is also part of this process: their care, cooking and cleaning enables the workers to survive.

Social reproduction theory examines the processes involved in creating and sustaining life in a capitalist society. It looks at the connections between the labour used to produce goods and services, and the labour (both paid and unpaid) that is needed outside the workplace to create this labour force and keep it going.

Feminist activists and scholars have drawn attention to this unpaid labour, calling for strikes, collective action and class solidarity.

THE WORKING CLASS INCLUDES EVERYONE IN THE PRODUCING CLASS INVOLVED IN THE REPRODUCTION OF SOCIETY – WHETHER PAID OR UNPAID. THIS VISION OF CLASS GATHERS TOGETHER THE TEMPORARY LATINX HOTEL WORKER FROM LOS ANGELES, THE FLEXTIME WORKING MOTHER FROM INDIANA WHO NEEDS TO STAY HOME DUE TO HIGH CHILDCARE COSTS, THE AFRICAN AMERICAN FULL-TIME SCHOOL TEACHER FROM CHICAGO, AND THE WHITE, MALE, UNEMPLOYED FORMER CAR FACTORY WORKER FROM DETROIT. THEY COME TOGETHER NOT IN COMPETITION WITH EACH OTHER BUT IN SOLIDARITY.

HISTORIAN TITHI BHATTACHARYA

ACROSS THE WORLD, WOMEN ARE ON STRIKE. THE WOMEN'S STRIKE IS ABOUT REALIZING THE POWER WE ALREADY HOLD – IT IS OUR LABOUR THAT KEEPS THE WORLD TURNING AND PROFITS FLOWING. WHEN WE STOP, THE WORLD STOPS WITH US.

PAYING FOR DOMESTIC LABOUR

Feminist thinkers have questioned the ethics of employing domestic workers, arguing that the emancipation of women from housework is often reliant on the exploitation of lower-class and immigrant women.

In their research conducted in France, sociologists Christelle Avril and Marie Cartier argue that not only is domestic work founded upon the triple inequalities of gender, race and class, but that the work itself leads to the subordination of employees:

1. Much domestic work is "live-in" with poorly defined boundaries between work and private life.
2. Working within the private sphere puts workers at greater risk of poor treatment.
3. Domestic workers often provide care, requiring high levels of emotional labour.
4. Domestic work lacks regulation, and many domestic workers do not have an employment contract or identity papers.

Marketing academic Rohit Varman and colleagues conducted research with female domestic service providers in India. They suggest that high-status clients follow norms of consumption without questioning the ethics of their interactions with domestic workers. Exploitation occurs within everyday relations between those who consume and those who serve, and this plays a role in reproducing inequalities based on class, caste and gender.

THE PRECARIAT

In 2014 Guy Standing argued that the precariat is a new global social class of people whose working lives are insecure. This includes people with short-term contracts, lack of employment rights and no stable income. It also includes people with permanent contracts who face insecurity in the workplace – such as being moved from job to job by managers in the same company. The precariat differs from classifications based on occupation type or socio-economic position, and can include people with very different backgrounds and access to resources.

THE TEENAGER SURVIVING ON FLEETING JOBS IS NOT THE SAME AS THE MIGRANT WHO USES HIS WITS TO SURVIVE, NETWORKING FEVERISHLY WHILE WORRYING ABOUT THE POLICE. NEITHER IS SIMILAR TO THE SINGLE MOTHER FRETTING WHERE THE MONEY FOR NEXT WEEK'S FOOD BILL IS COMING FROM OR THE MAN IN HIS 60S WHO TAKES CASUAL JOBS TO HELP PAY MEDICAL BILLS. BUT THEY ALL SHARE A SENSE THAT THEIR LABOUR IS INSTRUMENTAL (TO LIVE), OPPORTUNISTIC (TAKING WHAT COMES) AND PRECARIOUS (INSECURE).

ECONOMIST GUY STANDING

63

THE GIG ECONOMY

Mobile apps for services such as courier delivery and taxi driving are part of a "gig economy" made up of insecure work organized through online platforms. The apps connect the worker to a person paying for the "gig". The companies running the platforms, such as food delivery service Deliveroo, often classify the workers as "self-employed". This means they have fewer employment rights and protections than staff employed directly by a company – even in cases where the company organizes the way that the work is done (such as setting the price of the service and the hours of work).

THE NEW YORK TAXI WORKERS ALLIANCE AND THE INDEPENDENT WORKERS UNION OF GREAT BRITAIN HAVE WON GAINS IN PAY RATES AND WORKING CONDITIONS. THE GMB UNION WON A CASE TO RECLASSIFY UBER DRIVERS AS "WORKERS". THIS GAVE 30,000 DRIVERS IN THE UK ACCESS TO HOLIDAY PAY, MINIMUM WAGE AND BREAKS.

GEOGRAPHER HANNAH JOHNSTON AND LABOUR RELATIONS SPECIALIST CHRIS LAND-KAZLAUSKAS, ILO

WE HAVE TO ACCEPT JOBS NOT KNOWING WHAT THEY ARE OR HOW MUCH WE'LL GET PAID. THEY CAN SACK US WITHOUT ANY REAL EXPLANATION.

The International Labour Organization (ILO) explored different collective strategies used by gig economy workers to push for better rights. These include legal challenges by trade unions on the classification of workers, the formation of new grassroots unions and the development of workers' co-operatives.

THE GREAT BRITISH CLASS SURVEY

The Great British Class Survey was carried out in 2011 by the BBC, along with a group of academics. 161,400 people completed the survey, making it the biggest study of social class in Britain. Mike Savage, Fiona Devine, Niall Cunningham, Mark Taylor, Yaojun Li, Johs Hjellbrekke, Brigitte Le Roux, Sam Friedman and Andrew Miles combined these findings with other data on social class to develop a new set of seven class categories.

ELITE
ESTABLISHED MIDDLE CLASS
TECHNICAL MIDDLE CLASS
NEW AFFLUENT WORKERS
TRADITIONAL WORKING CLASS
EMERGENT SERVICE WORKERS
PRECARIAT

WE'RE NOT SEEKING TO DEVELOP A BETTER OCCUPATIONAL OR EMPLOYMENT-BASED MEASURE OF CLASS. RATHER, OUR MODEL IS DESIGNED TO SHED MORE LIGHT ON CULTURAL AND SOCIAL BOUNDARIES IN BRITAIN AND HOW THIS MIGHT SUGGEST NEW LINES OF CLASS DIVISION.

GBCS SOCIOLOGISTS

This analysis of class draws on Pierre Bourdieu's theory of capitals, exploring the relationship between our social class and different kinds of resources such as money, wealth, social links and cultural knowledge. For more information about these ideas see pages 39-40.

THE "ORDINARY" ELITE

Popular representations of the elite tend to fall into two categories: the aristocrat and the businessman. Cultural markers of class are different across time and space, but they often centre on evidence of inherited status (such as property or access to particular networks of people) or visible signs of wealth (such as expensive goods). However, the dominance of these figures in popular culture – from *Downton Abbey* to *The Apprentice* – may in fact distract us from the "ordinary" wealthy. The Great British Class Survey revealed an Elite who extended far beyond the 1%, suggesting extremely affluent households make up 6% of British society. The researchers found that not everyone who fit within this new category was comfortable with the idea of being part of an "elite".

THE CLASS CEILING

Britain's high-status professions in law, medicine, engineering and journalism continue to be dominated by the privately educated privileged class. But what about those who do manage to scale the social mobility ladder? How successful are the upwardly mobile once they enter elite professions? Is there a "class ceiling" blocking the accumulation of wealth for those from working-class backgrounds?

Sociologists Sam Friedman and Daniel Laurison's research suggests there is a difference between elite professions, with "traditional" jobs remaining more exclusive than "emerging" roles in areas such as IT; even when the upwardly mobile are successful in entering elite professions, they have lower incomes than their colleagues from more privileged backgrounds.

Sociologist Maren Toft also worked with Friedman to explore the "class ceiling" in Norway. They argue that parental wealth plays a central role in the education and work trajectories of elite professionals. This includes funds for private tutoring, a "safety net" for internships and unpaid work, capital for housing, and gifts from family that are used for investments.

STUDYING SURNAME PERSISTENCE AMONG OXBRIDGE GRADUATES AND HOLDERS OF TOP POSITIONS SINCE THE 13TH CENTURY, I BELIEVE SOCIAL STATUS IN BRITAIN IS MORE STRONGLY INHERITED THAN HEIGHT.

ECONOMIST GREGORY CLARK

FLOW OF CAPITAL AMONG GLOBAL ELITES

In *Capital in the Twenty-First Century*, economist Thomas Piketty distinguishes the unequal distribution of income from the unequal distribution of inherited wealth, arguing that the latter drives capital accumulation. Therefore, kinship continues to play a central role in capitalist society.

THIS MEANS THAT ACCUMULATED WEALTH CONTINUES TO GROW AT A RATE THAT OUTSTRIPS THE GROWTH OF WAGES AND SALARIES.

THE CENTRAL CONTRADICTION OF CAPITALISM

RETURN ON CAPITAL > ECONOMIC GROWTH RATE

ACCUMULATED WEALTH

WAGES

"KEY WORKERS"

The efforts of "key workers" during the Covid-19 pandemic, which began in 2019, were publicly celebrated across the world. Alongside traditionally higher-status workers, such as doctors and teachers, those providing essential services, such as carers, supermarket staff, refuse collectors, people working in food production and cleaners were identified as key workers.

I HAD ANOTHER ATTEMPT AT GETTING THROUGH TO UNIVERSAL CREDIT TODAY. I DON'T HAVE A COMPUTER SO I NEED TO SPEAK TO SOMEONE ON THE PHONE AND IT'S A NIGHTMARE. OH MY GOD! WHY CAN'T SOMEONE JUST ANSWER THE PHONE?

OVERCROWDING IS ON MY MIND EVERY MINUTE AND IT KEEPS ME AWAKE AT NIGHT. I STAY CALM IN FRONT OF THE CHILDREN BUT I AM GETTING WORRIED NOW. IT'S ALSO BECOMING CLEAR THAT BLACK PEOPLE ARE MUCH MORE AT RISK OF CATCHING COVID, WHICH IS HEARTBREAKING AND DEVASTATING FOR US ALL TO LEARN.

Many of these essential professions have not been valued in the past and are poorly paid. The Joseph Rowntree Foundation, an organization working to solve poverty in the UK, asked key workers to keep a diary documenting how the pandemic affected their life. They found that families were living in cramped housing, working long unsociable hours for poverty wages and facing difficulties accessing welfare support.

UNEMPLOYMENT AND "WORKLESSNESS"

In capitalist societies, paid work is one of the main ways that people meet their needs and survive. Although many of us are involved in activities that could be described as "work" (such as caring for others, making or fixing things), paid employment tends to be more highly regarded. Dominant stories about the importance of being employed combine religious and moral ideas about "work ethic" with neoliberal economic policies.

IN THE UK, THE PUBLIC ARE TOLD THAT YOU ARE ONLY SEEN AS A CITIZEN THROUGH WORK. THE GOVERNMENT CUT SUPPORT FOR PEOPLE OUT OF WORK. THIS IS BASED ON THE MYTH THAT DEPRIVED PEOPLE DON'T WORK (OR DON'T WANT TO).

SOCIOLOGIST IMOGEN TYLER

WE REGRET TO INFORM YOU THAT YOUR APPLICATION WAS NOT SUCCESSFUL.

THE PROBLEM HERE IS A LACK OF ASPIRATION AND DRIVE.

CLOSED

Researchers Robert MacDonald, Tracy Shildrick, Colin Webster and Kayleigh Garthwaite argue that being trapped in a low-pay no-pay cycle, in and out of insecure jobs and unemployment, can keep people in poverty. Employment does not necessarily lift people out.

THE WELFARE STATE

Publicly-funded services (such as education and healthcare) and state-organized systems of social insurance (such as financial support when people are unable to do paid work) exist in different forms across the world. Within capitalist societies, welfare provisions are often presented as a buffer between the market and the population. As we heard from David Harvey earlier in the book (see page 46), the global rise of neoliberalism has driven widespread cuts to public spending and an attack on the idea of welfare provisions. These economic policies have an impact on the formation and representation of social class.

Current political and media discourse justifies the inequalities of neoliberalism by presenting poverty as an individual issue – a product of "bad choices" or laziness, rather than of structural inequality.

THE FIGURE OF CRISIS IN TODAY'S WELFARE DEBATE IS THE IMAGINED "SKIVER". THROUGH INVENTING ANXIETIES ABOUT THE SCHEMING DECEITS OF THOSE ENTITLED TO SOCIAL PROTECTION, SUCH ENTITLEMENTS BECOME EASIER TO UNDERMINE AND DISMANTLE. THIS RESTS ON A DISTINCTION BETWEEN "SKIVERS" AND "STRIVERS" — WHICH IMAGINES THAT THE POPULATION CAN BE CLEAVED INTO TWO CLEAR GROUPS, THOSE WHO WORK ("PUT IN TO THE SYSTEM") AND THOSE WHO DON'T ("TAKE OUT OF THE SYSTEM").

SOCIOLOGIST TRACEY JENSEN

ANOTHER LIE-IN...

STRUCTURAL ADJUSTMENT PROGRAMMES

The cuts to public spending and welfare that David Harvey talks about have been felt across the world – in neoliberal national economic policies and via **structural adjustment programmes** since the 1970s. This involves the International Monetary Fund (IMF) and World Bank loaning money on the condition that the borrowing country make policy reforms, often in favour of free market economics. These might include the privatization of previously state-funded public services, austerity (cuts to public spending) and **deregulation** of the labour market, such as reducing wages and workers' rights.

THE PRISON INDUSTRIAL COMPLEX

Scholar and activist Angela Davis argues that imprisonment is increasingly used by national governments as a response to social issues that could be better addressed by social support and welfare programmes. The USA has the highest rate of incarceration in the world, with Black and Latinx people disproportionately represented in the prison population.

The institution of policing in southern US states has roots in slave patrols of the 18th century. These patrols searched for and forcibly "returned" or punished people who had escaped or resisted slavery.

The **prison industrial complex** is a concept that explores the role of prison in the capitalist system – pointing to the prison system and industries around imprisonment (such as those providing transport, surveillance and food), in which companies profit from the arrest and incarceration of people. Prisons can also be places where work and production are carried out for low cost, with incarcerated people forced to work for little pay.

CLASS CONSCIOUSNESS

Marx argued that classes are created through struggle. As workers come to understand their common experiences and common interests, they join together against capital, and so form a "class for itself" – consciously acting together politically to transform the structure of society. This might take the form of collective organization in the workplace and local communities, and solidarity and learning between working-class people globally.

Consciousness-raising involves people learning about the **social** aspects of the issues they face – and seeing how these connect up to other people's struggles across the world. Revolutionaries, social justice activists and campaigners often learn together about inequality through meetings, talks, social media, reading groups and publications.

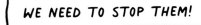

CHAPTER 4: LAND

Access to land and the resources that come from the land (such as minerals, water or food) has an impact on which groups have power in society and their relationship to each other. Land ownership has a bloody history – from the violent enslavement of people working on plantations in the Roman Empire or British colonies, to the expulsion and eviction of subsistence farmers and social tenants. In this chapter we'll explore some of the links between land, housing and social class.

THE ARISTOCRACY IN ENGLAND

The connection between land and class is strong and persistent in England. Guy Shrubsole has been investigating and mapping out who currently owns England – a surprisingly difficult task, as not all land is registered. He suggests that a third of England is still owned by families who have passed down large areas of land to their eldest son for generations. This land was often originally gained through violence or gifted by others who had seized it. The proceeds from colonialism and slavery were ploughed into the development of many of these aristocratic estates – as well as grand buildings in cities like London and Liverpool.

MANY OF THE ARISTOCRATIC FAMILIES WHO CONTINUE TO PROSPER AND OWN GREAT SWATHES OF THE UK CAN DATE THEIR BLOODLINES ALL THE WAY BACK TO THE NORMAN CONQUEST. INDEED, SOME OF THE LARGEST LANDOWNERS IN ENGLAND TODAY OWE THEIR TERRITORIAL EMPIRES TO THE PATRONAGE OF WILLIAM THE CONQUEROR.

WRITER AND CAMPAIGNER GUY SHRUBSOLE

THIS IS THE PERFECT SPOT FOR OUR NEW LUXURY FLATS.

THIS IS SOCIAL CLEANSING!

THERE ARE 141 COUNCIL TENANTS LIVING HERE!

NOT FOR LONG!

THE ENCLOSURE OF LAND

Land is a valuable resource, and there has always been a relationship between power and who has access to and use of land. However, land has not always been considered property. Historians refer to the process of the privatization of common land, and the removal of rights to the communal use of resources from the land, as "**enclosure**". This began in around the 15th century and has played a crucial role in class formation and class relations.

REMOVING THE ABILITY TO LIVE OFF COMMON LAND MEANT THAT WORKERS BECAME MORE DEPENDENT ON WAGED LABOUR TO SURVIVE. THIS GAVE EMPLOYERS THE POWER TO CUT PAY AND LENGTHEN THE WORKING DAY.

SCHOLAR AND ACTIVIST SILVIA FEDERICI

Anti-enclosure action has been a site of class struggle around the world since then – whether against the aristocracy, colonizers or transnational corporations. For example, in 17th-century England the Diggers set up camps to dig land, calling for common use and redistribution. Since the 1990s, Ogoni women in Nigeria have used nonviolent resistance in their fight against oil drilling and its exploitation of people, environment and resources.

YOU HAVE STOLEN OUR LAND – POISONED OUR AIR AND WATER.

POLLUTION KILLS

POLICING THE LAND

Political theorist Mark Neocleous argues that this process of separating workers from land and resources was fundamental in the development of capitalism. In emerging capitalist states, laws and violent policing forced people off land and out of homes. Those who tried to live outside of the wage system were criminalized as "vagrants".

POLICE POWER WAS A CENTRAL FORCE IN THE DEVELOPMENT OF A CLASS OF WAGE LABOURERS.

MARK NEOCLEOUS

Vagrancy laws, which were first developed in England from the 14th century, were transported globally via colonialism. The way that these laws have been interpreted and used varies across countries and time periods – many are still in operation now. What they share in common is that they are generally used to police marginalized groups, are focused on the maintenance of "order" and are broad in scope – whether in preventing the movement of people from one place to another, restricting where people can gather or sleep, or punishing people who are out of work.

PRIVATIZATION OF THE COMMONS

"**Commons**" are land or resources which belong to the community. They can become commodified through private ownership and used to make profit. For instance, water can be viewed as a **commodity** or as part of the commons.

As a commodity, water is like any other essential good or service: private companies respond to customers and shareholders by efficiently providing water, incentivizing conservation and profitably managing supply systems.

ALL FIXED, AND I'VE ADDED A TIMER THAT'LL HELP YOU USE LESS WATER AND SAVE MONEY ON YOUR BILLS!

When viewed as part of the commons, water is an essential resource that cannot be substituted for another product and that is connected to communities through the hydrological cycle. Water supply is often subject to market and state failures, and so many people argue that communities are best placed to manage it in order to protect environmental and public health.

Following the Eurozone crisis (2009–14), austerity was imposed upon five member states including Greece as a condition of financial bailouts from parties such as the IMF; much like structural adjustment programmes (page 73), this included public spending cuts and privatization.

Political economists Andreas Bieler and Jamie Jordan note that workers fought back against this. In May 2014 a city-wide referendum saw 98% of voters in Thessaloniki reject the proposed privatization of water and sanitation services.

NEW ENCLOSURES

The term "enclosure" has been used by many theorists to describe ongoing processes of privatization of the commons and the exclusion and displacement of people from it. Writing about the historical English enclosures, Marx labelled these "land grabs". This phrase has also been used in the present day in reference to large corporate land and resource acquisitions globally.

Much has been written about the privatization of public resources in Britain since Margaret Thatcher took power in 1979. Publicly owned railways, utilities, housing, education and the postal service have all been sold, often at a loss to the British taxpayer.

However, the biggest privatization of all has largely gone unnoticed. Facing little protest, the state has been selling vast quantities of public land to the private sector. Social geographer Brett Christophers uses the term "new enclosure" to describe land privatization in post-1970s Britain, drawing attention to the connection between contemporary privatization of land and the original enclosure Marx wrote about. Since 1979, 2 million hectares – that's about 10% of the entire British land mass – have moved from public to private hands. In today's prices, this land is likely to be worth around £400 billion.

CAPITALISM AND THE ENVIRONMENT

The current ecological crisis has highlighted the consequences of our consumption practices. However, the environmental damage caused by capitalist cycles of production and consumption is not a new idea. In 1867 Marx argued that capitalism causes a metabolic rift within nature by imposing a system where the nutrients of the soil are removed without being replaced.

Capitalist modes of production such as intensive farming not only fail to replenish the rural soil that feeds urban consumption but rely on robbing the soil resources of other countries too.

Sociologists Brett Clark and John Bellamy Foster call this process **ecological imperialism**, where imperial powers grow at unsustainable rates through the exploitation of the environment and consequent ecological degradation of other countries.

COBALT SUPPLY CHAIN

Cobalt is a metal used in the manufacturing of electronic goods such as smartphones and tablets.

Workers in a cobalt mine in the Democratic Republic of the Congo are paid as little as $0.65 (50p) a day to rinse stones to sell to traders.

"Buying houses" buy the cobalt from miners, process it and sell it on to manufacturing companies at a huge profit. The market price of cobalt spiked 300% from 2016–18 and continues to increase.

Cobalt is a key element of lithium-ion rechargeable batteries and is used by multinational technology companies in their products.

We use these products every time we send an email, check social media or drive an electric car.

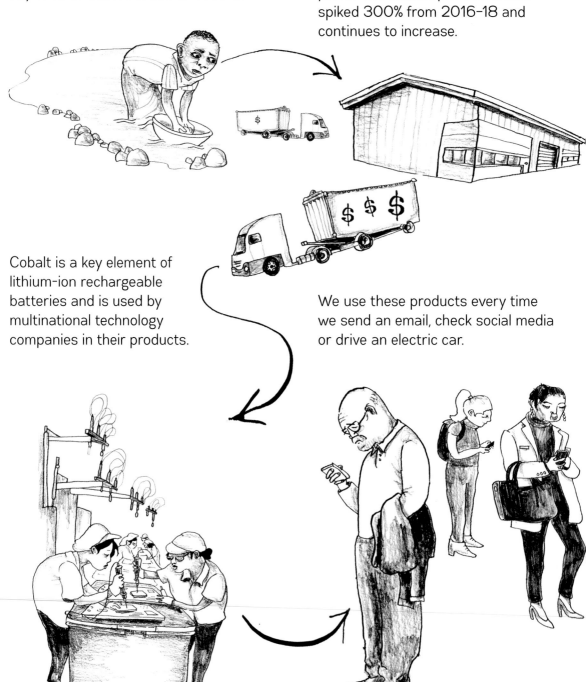

PRIVATE PROPERTY

FROM THE STANDPOINT OF A HIGHER ECONOMIC FORM OF SOCIETY, PRIVATE OWNERSHIP OF THE GLOBE BY SINGLE INDIVIDUALS WILL APPEAR QUITE AS ABSURD AS PRIVATE OWNERSHIP OF ONE MAN BY ANOTHER.

KARL MARX

Should there be such a thing as private property rights?

PROPERTY RIGHTS ARE AN IMPORTANT PART OF PERSONAL FREEDOM AND AUTONOMY; THEY MEAN I CAN DO WHAT I WANT WITHOUT HAVING TO SEEK APPROVAL FROM THE STATE OR ANYONE ELSE.

PROPERTY RIGHTS PLAY A CENTRAL ROLE IN CREATING A SOCIETY THAT PURSUES THE INTERESTS OF CAPITAL ACCUMULATION AT THE EXPENSE OF WORKING PEOPLE; THEY MEAN THAT I HAVE LESS RIGHTS IN MY OWN HOME THAN YOU DO.

THE HOUSING QUESTION

Housing shortages are often talked about in terms of "crisis", but they're not new. In the 1870s, philosopher Friedrich Engels argued that all oppressed classes in all periods of history suffer from poor housing. The stark housing inequalities of his time led some to argue that homeownership among the proletariat would have revolutionary potential.

TENANTS' RENTS SHOULD BE CONVERTED INTO PURCHASE PAYMENTS; THIS WILL END THE EXPLOITATIVE RELATIONSHIP BETWEEN LANDLORDS AND TENANTS.

PHILOSOPHER PIERRE-JOSEPH PROUDHON (1809–65) FOUNDED THE ECONOMIC THEORY OF MUTUALISM AND IS CONSIDERED THE "FATHER OF ANARCHISM".

HOME-AND-GARDEN OWNERSHIP WILL TRANSFORM WORKERS INTO CAPITALISTS, ENABLING THEM TO GENERATE INCOME AND IMPROVING THEIR SELF WORTH.

ECONOMIST AND SOCIAL REFORMER EMIL SAX (1845–1927)

But for Engels, poor housing conditions are just one of the many evils caused by capitalism, and the only real solution is for workers to expropriate private property. The abolition of capitalism would enable a conception of house and home that is of "use value" over "exchange value", and of shelter over profit: housing as a basic ecological need.

I CAN'T BELIEVE THAT BIG HOUSE SITS EMPTY ALL WINTER!

BUT HOLIDAY HOMES DO MAKE A LOT OF MONEY IN THE SUMMER MONTHS.

WHAT ABOUT THE FAMILIES WHO NEED A HOME ALL YEAR ROUND?!

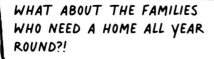

HOUSING INEQUALITY

Housing inequality does not just entrench wealth polarization, it draws a line between those who have access to the safety and security of a home and those who do not. This is the consequence of two connected inequalities: **housing wealth** and **housing tenure**.

Housing is the largest component of national wealth, so growing inequalities in housing wealth shape inequalities of wealth more broadly. House price inflation, and the consequent inequality between those who own their home and those who do not, is the result of:

• The idealization of home ownership as a financial investment.

THIS IS AN UP-AND-COMING AREA – THE FLAT WILL ONLY INCREASE IN VALUE!

• The expansion and deregulation of mortgage finance.

• Generous tax policies subsidizing home ownership.

HOUSE PRICES KEEP RISING AND I'LL BE ABLE TO SELL AT A PROFIT WITHOUT PAYING CAPITAL GAINS TAX. FINALLY, I'LL BE ABLE TO AFFORD MY DREAM HOME!

"Tenure" refers to the economic arrangements under which you have the right to live in a property. Tenure inequality is based on the privileging of owner occupation above other forms of tenure (such as private and social rent). This has material and social effects; rental tenures are insecure, with poorer housing conditions and a source of stigma.

While the share of income going to labour (in the form of wages and benefits) has shrunk globally since the 1980s, a small minority have been able to accumulate vast wealth, not through production, but from rental income. "Rentiers" are those who gain their income from the ownership of property (financial, physical and intellectual) rather than from labour. Economist Guy Standing argues that rentiers have become the main beneficiaries of this emerging capitalist income distribution system.

HOUSING AND CLASSIFICATION

Architecture, tenure and location are used in cultural representations to talk about class. These classifications of place shape the social conditions of life (how we feel and how others treat us because of where we live) and transform the material environment (the quality and type of housing and local services). From the disinvestment in council housing in the UK to the racially discriminatory mortgage lending practice of redlining in the USA, neighbourhood decline must be understood as a consequence of broader processes, such as housing policies and practices.

Redlining is a discriminatory practice of not offering services to certain locations based on the ethnicity or race of the population in the area. In the USA in the 1930s, mortgage risk was calculated partly on the basis of maps which labelled areas with higher proportions of Black residents as "hazardous".

HOUSING STIGMA

The sociologist Loïc Wacquant called the social classification of places "territorial stigmatization". Stigma based on where you live has been documented in ghettos in the United States, traditional working-class territories within and on the peripheries of European cities, and urban segregation in Latin America.

Within the UK, territorial stigmatization is exemplified in media and political representations of the "sink estate". Social scientist Simone van de Wetering suggests that, rather than simply internalizing stigma, residents do not accept their "deviant" label and use strategies to rework existing norms, extending what is considered "normal" to include their experiences.

THE "SINK ESTATE" HAS BECOME A SEMANTIC BATTERING RAM IN THE IDEOLOGICAL ASSAULT ON SOCIAL HOUSING.

URBAN GEOGRAPHER TOM SLATER

THESE FAMILIES ARE A DISGRACE!

HOW MANY KIDS HAS SHE GOT?!

DO ANY OF THEM HAVE A JOB?!

WELCOME TO THE SINK ESTATE

HOSTILE ARCHITECTURE

Public space is designed to encourage particular behaviour. Take, for example, the removal of the curb between the road and the pedestrian path, which seeks to slow drivers down. Or the ridges on a two-way cycle path which act as a physical reminder of which is the correct side to ride. Such architecture can encourage behaviour that increases co-operation and community safety. However, it is often used coercively in an increasingly securitized urban context, "designing out" certain identities, behaviours and categories of people from public places.

Although there has been public outcry about the use of hostile architecture in many cities worldwide – such as anti-homeless spikes on benches or under bridges – criminologist James Petty argues this may reflect the public's distaste towards the homeless rather than real resistance to exclusionary structures. He argues that the spikes act as a visible reminder of both the homeless people they remove and the violent mechanisms used to control them.

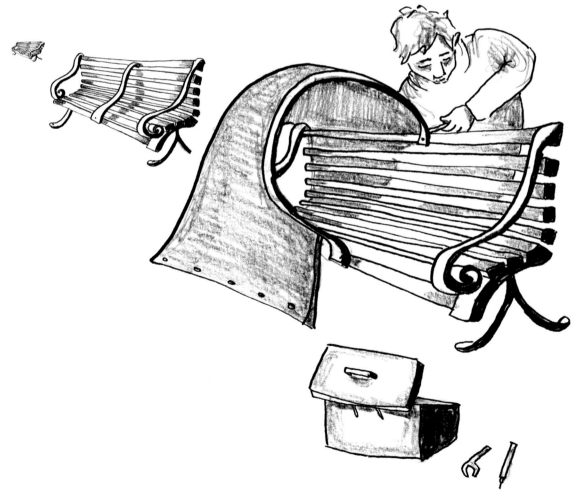

GENTRIFICATION

Gentrification is a process of redevelopment which aims to tackle environmental, economic and social problems by attracting capital to less affluent areas. Middle-class settlement is assumed to enhance poorer communities, as the social and economic capital they bring with them is invested in the local area. However, research has shown that gentrification does not always lead to mixed communities, rather that the middle class often remain segregated, both in terms of their residence and the services they use.

The urban geographer Andrea Mösgen argues that the role of the state has shifted from securing affordable housing for low-income households into becoming an essential player in real estate speculation. Stigmatization of both the people and the place justifies disinvestment and helps to make the site ripe for future investment of capital. State-led gentrification refers to the role of the state in governing gentrification and displacement in areas previously thought to be unattractive for profit-seeking capital.

GENTRIFICATION RESISTANCE

Resistance to gentrification refers to the practices of individuals and groups who try to stay put in the face of rising social and financial exclusion within their community. Human geographers Sandra Annunziata and Clara Rivas-Alonso suggest that our definition of resistance must include both politically conscious, overtly oppositional, intentional and visible practices as well as non-politicized, covert, unintentional, informal and deliberately invisible practices of everyday life.

As such, many acts of anti-gentrification resistance remain relatively invisible, as rather than taking the form of mass social movements, they are enacted through daily micro-practices. Research by social scientists María Carla Rodríguez and María Mercedes Di Virgilio explains how in Latin American cities, resistance can take the form of popular survival practices such as squatting, informal employment or informal housing.

The 2001 financial crisis in Argentina led to the expansion of the anti-eviction movement in Buenos Aires. Many co-operatives were organized among families living in tenements or squatting in abandoned buildings.

ANTI-CAPITALIST HOUSING POLITICS

In this chapter we have seen how the privatization of land is central to the formation and maintenance of class inequalities. From the enclosure of the commons to the accumulation of wealth through property ownership, capitalism is founded upon the commodification of land. However, there are alternative visions of housing that can disrupt capitalism.

Marxists believe that workers, not tenants, are the agents of change in capitalist society, through working-class revolution and expropriation of private property.

CAPITALISM EXPLOITS US AT WORK AND AT HOME. WE NEED A NEW SYSTEM WHERE OUR CONTRIBUTIONS TO SOCIETY ARE VALUED AND RESOURCES ARE SHARED EQUALLY.

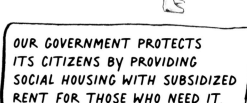

OUR GOVERNMENT PROTECTS ITS CITIZENS BY PROVIDING SOCIAL HOUSING WITH SUBSIDIZED RENT FOR THOSE WHO NEED IT.

Socialists emphasize the strategic importance of state intervention, for example, council housing.

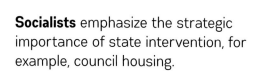

IT'S UNFAIR THAT LANDLORDS LEAVE PROPERTIES EMPTY WHEN THERE IS SUCH A HIGH NEED FOR HOUSING! AS SQUATTERS WE BELIEVE HOMES NEED PEOPLE TO LIVE IN THEM.

Anarchists champion local control, autonomy and self-organized solutions in the here and now, such as small-scale co-operatives and mutual ownership.

CHAPTER 5: CULTURE

"Culture" refers to the beliefs, practices and objects that make up our way of life. Culture connects our past, present and future. Your cultural background will shape your behaviour today, in turn producing the cultural norms of the future.

Culture is made up of thoughts (non-material culture) and things (material culture) and is organized through cultural practices: the rules and logic we use when going about our everyday life.

In this next chapter we will explore different ideas about the relationship between culture and social class.

CLASS AND CULTURE

> IDEAS, BELIEFS, ART AND ARTIFACTS REPRODUCE AND LEGITIMATE THE INEQUALITIES OF WEALTH AND POWER IN CAPITALIST SOCIETY.

SOCIOLOGIST DAVID GARTMAN

There is general agreement among class theorists that culture helps to create and justify class inequality. But there is disagreement about how this happens.

Pierre Bourdieu argued that cultural objects are ranked, and therefore classes are distinguished by their different cultures, with some being seen as superior to others. This hierarchy of culture justifies unequal distributions of power and wealth. The dominant class are believed to consume the "right" culture and therefore seem to deserve their privileged positions, whereas the dominated class consume the "wrong" culture, explaining their lower positions.

Rather than cultural differences, the **Frankfurt School** – a philosophical and sociological tradition founded in the 1930s – argued that it is cultural similarity which masks the real class divisions in society. Mass culture is consumed by everyone in modern society. This creates the illusion that everyone in society is the same and therefore equal. Although some have more of what everyone wants, this is accepted as it is believed that hard work is rewarded with a higher wage.

> SEE, EVEN THE PRIME MINISTER SUPPORTS ARSENAL!

MIDDLE-CLASS DOMINATION

Bourdieu argues that the dominant middle class do not simply accumulate economic capital but also **cultural capital**: cultural objects, beliefs and practices that are valued in society. Highbrow culture, such as classic literature, art, ballet and opera, is valuable to the middle class because it can be converted into other forms of capital.

For example, if you have lots of money you might be able to buy a famous work of art. Ownership gives you cultural capital in the **objectified state**: by displaying art in your home you can communicate your highbrow culture to visitors.

However, money can't buy "good taste", and so you also need to understand what is considered art and what is not. This knowledge is cultural capital in the **embodied state**: it shapes your likes and dislikes and so is believed to be a personal preference rather than something learned.

Children born into families who own highbrow cultural objects or attend cultural events develop knowledge of this culture. When they go to school, this understanding is taken to be intelligence. So education enables the middle class to exchange their cultural capital for educational qualifications. Once cultural capital is in this **institutionalized state**, it can be cashed in for economic capital through access to highly paid jobs.

THE MYTH OF MERITOCRACY

The "American Dream" is a belief system dominant in the USA and in many Western capitalist societies. This commonly held idea suggests that you get out of life what you put in, so your position in society is determined by your individual merit. The American Dream is based on the idea of a **meritocracy**; if you work hard and have a high ability, you will do well.

Meritocracy is often tied to arguments about **social mobility** – the idea that people's resources and circumstances can change over time, such as moving "up" in occupational class or social status. The World Economic Forum has argued that there is stark inequality in most countries and that only a small number have policies and conditions that support social mobility.

THE IDEA OF MERITOCRACY ACTS AS AN ALIBI FOR THE WEALTHY ELITE. IT JUSTIFIES THE WEALTH OF THE RICH AND TELLS INDIVIDUALS THEY CAN OVERCOME INEQUALITY THROUGH INDIVIDUALISM AND COMPETITION.

SOCIOLOGIST JO LITTLER

IT'S TAKEN HARD WORK, BUT I ALWAYS BELIEVED I WOULD SUCCEED.

BUSINESS PERSON OF THE YEAR

THE ONLY THING THAT STOPS YOU FROM ACHIEVING YOUR DREAMS IS YOU.

New Luxury Apartments

A common challenge to the idea of meritocracy is inheritance. It provides many non-merit advantages. If you are born into a wealthy family you will be brought up with the safety and security of decent housing; you will have access to educational opportunities which will help you identify and cultivate personal merit; you will have the safety net of cash, property and opportunity if you ever face personal crisis or failure; and you will have access to better healthcare, consequently living a longer and healthier life.

MERITOCRACY IS A MYTH. WHAT WE OFTEN CONSIDER "MERIT" FACTORS ARE NOT AS UNIQUELY INDIVIDUAL OR AS INFLUENTIAL AS WE THINK. NON-MERIT FACTORS SUCH AS INHERITANCE, SOCIAL AND CULTURAL ADVANTAGES, UNEQUAL EDUCATIONAL OPPORTUNITY AND DISCRIMINATION IN ALL OF ITS FORMS IMPACT OUR SOCIAL POSITION.

SOCIOLOGISTS STEPHEN J. MCNAMEE AND ROBERT K. MILLER JR.

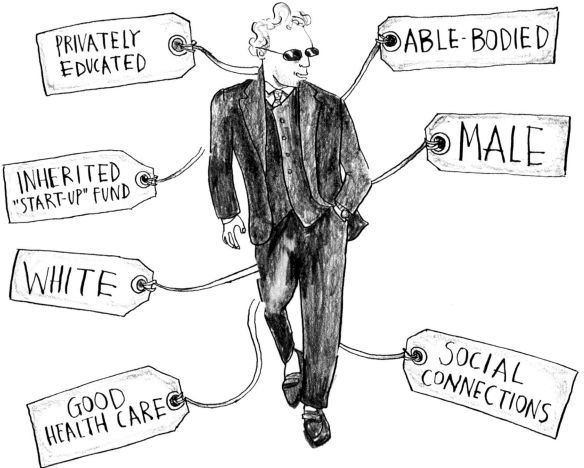

CHILDHOOD

Sociologist Annette Lareau's 2011 research with American families found different cultural practices of child rearing between middle-class and working-class parents. For middle-class parents, it was important to invest time and money in cultural activities outside of school. These parents engaged in the "concerted cultivation" of their children's future skill set. For working-class parents, it was important that their children accomplished "natural growth" and so their children engaged with more "childlike" activities. Clear boundaries were drawn between childhood and adulthood with children allowed to direct their own play and leisure activities.

Middle-class children therefore often gain the skills valued within education and work, while working-class children's experience is often out of sync with institutional expectations. These class differences in family life shape how children view themselves in relation to the rest of the world, with middle-class children developing a sense of entitlement and working-class children experiencing distance, distrust and constraint in their encounters with institutions.

SCHOOL

For sociologists Pierre Bourdieu and Jean-Claude Passeron, education is the key way that middle-class privilege is reproduced in society. They argue that schools impose middle-class culture on students, rewarding those who fit into these cultural practices and putting working-class children with a different culture at a disadvantage. This results in middle-class children being seen as "ideal learners" whereas working-class children are positioned as "anti-school".

Historian David Kynaston and economist Francis Green argue that within the UK, private education (where you pay fees to attend) is a key mechanism in the reproduction of privilege. Despite only educating one in every 16 pupils, private schools accumulate educational resources, with one in every 7 teachers working at a private school and £1 out of every £6 of school expenditure in England spent for the benefit of private-school pupils.

But there are class differences within state education too. Sociologist Diane Reay highlights how, even within the comprehensive system, different social classes are being educated for different functions in society. The application of market principles to education within the UK means that parents are encouraged to act as consumers and "choose" the school which is right for their child. Schools in wealthier areas tend to do well in exam result league tables as their pupils have the cultural advantages of coming from a middle-class family, so middle-class families will continue to "choose" this school. Because funding is allocated based on enrollment and exam success, these schools will be rewarded and have access to more resources than schools which are unpopular with middle-class parents.

HIGHER EDUCATION

Social class has an impact on access to higher education, and on people's experiences during and after university. Ideas about "social mobility" being available via further education miss the structural barriers and inequalities that many students face, including during the admissions process.

Education researchers Penny Jane Burke and Jackie McManus examined inequalities in admissions to art and design degrees in the UK. They explored the class prejudice and racism implicit in judgements interviewers were making about what counts as "legitimate" knowledge. In one case study, a Black working-class applicant wasn't given a place on a Fashion Design BA. The interviewers had rejected her because she was influenced by hip-hop. They also saw her intention to live at home as evidence of "immaturity" in contrast with more affluent applicants who planned to leave home.

DISGUST

Sociologists Steph Lawler and Imogen Tyler have explored the role that disgust plays in marking out the boundaries between classes. They both argue that class is dynamic and relational – something that is made and remade through interactions and representations.

> DISGUST PRESENTS WORKING-CLASS PEOPLE AS ABHORRENT AND AS FOUNDATIONALLY "OTHER" TO A MIDDLE-CLASS EXISTENCE THAT IS SILENTLY MARKED AS NORMAL AND DESIRABLE. BUT THE BOURGEOISIE ALSO WORK TO PRODUCE MIDDLE-CLASSED IDENTITIES THAT RELY ON NOT BEING THE REPELLENT AND DISGUSTING "OTHER".

STEPH LAWLER

> THE SCALE OF THE DISGUST DIRECTED AGAINST ASYLUM SEEKERS IS EXTRAORDINARY. THIS DISGUST IS USED TO CONSTITUTE THE BORDERS OF THE NATION STATE – BY MAKING SOME PEOPLE ILLEGAL – AND IS ALSO A FUNDAMENTAL ASPECT OF A NEW GLOBAL MARKET IN ASYLUM DETENTION AND DEPORTATION.

IMOGEN TYLER

CAREFUL! WHO KNOWS WHAT YOU MIGHT CATCH IF YOU FELL IN!

CONSTRUCTING THE "WHITE WORKING CLASS"

Since the global financial crash in 2008, it has been more commonplace in the UK and USA to see explicit discussions about social class in mainstream media. The most striking examples of this were the reporting and political commentary around the election of President Trump in 2016 in the USA, the "Leave" vote in the UK referendum on membership of the EU in the same year, and the 2019 UK general election.

Each of these political events was marked by discussion about the connection between social class and politics, and framed by arguments about the "White working class" as both "left behind" and "dangerous". Some of this discussion presented these votes as a "cultural divide" between the "White working class" and the "metropolitan elite". However, this simplified more complex issues of class identity, economic inequality and race.

THERE ARE NO JOBS AROUND HERE ANYMORE. THOSE RICH POLITICIANS ARE OUT OF TOUCH.

HEY! WORKING-CLASS PEOPLE AREN'T JUST WHITE!

THE NEWS

LABOUR PARTY LOSES WHITE WORKING-CLASS VOTES

HOW COULD WORKING-CLASS PEOPLE VOTE THIS WAY?!

THE FOCUS ON THE WHITE WORKING CLASS TENDS TO SIDESTEP OR DENY THE EXISTENCE OF THE "BLACK WORKING CLASS".

DIRECTOR OF TASO OMAR KHAN AND ECONOMIST FAIZA SHAHEEN

Political scientist Robbie Shilliam argues that the concept of the "White working class" has its historical roots in British Empire, and that distinctions between the "deserving" and "undeserving" poor have been racialized throughout British history. These distinctions have been central to ideas about who should have access to welfare and social support. This has changed over time and place, but Shilliam argues that the way the category has been defined has always been driven by the most powerful in society.

At the same time, the working class have always had a precarious relationship to Whiteness, often positioned as outside of middle-class White respectability or in contrast to "cosmopolitan" middle-class culture. This sets up a distinction between "uneducated" and "uncultured" masses and "educated" and "cosmopolitan" middle classes. In this context, the "White middle class" can use both their Whiteness and access to global cultures as resources, which is much less possible for working-class people.

MEDIA REPRESENTATION

Cultural and media scholars have drawn attention to the role that media plays in our understanding and experience of social class. Media representations are one way that stories about society are shared between people. Images, language and sound can all work together in different ways to produce meaning about class – whether in documentaries, music, news reports, social media posts, adverts or Hollywood blockbusters.

THAT WAS A REVOLUTIONARY FILM ABOUT BLACK LIBERATION.

NO, THE FILM TREATS BLACK AMERICAN MEN AS DISPOSABLE.

WE GIVE THINGS MEANING BY HOW WE REPRESENT THEM — THE WORDS WE USE ABOUT THEM, THE STORIES WE TELL ABOUT THEM, THE IMAGES OF THEM WE PRODUCE, THE EMOTIONS WE ASSOCIATE WITH THEM, THE WAYS WE CLASSIFY AND CONCEPTUALIZE THEM, THE VALUES WE PLACE ON THEM.

CULTURAL THEORIST STUART HALL

TALKING ABOUT CELEBRITIES

Media representations of social class aren't one-way. We talk about the things that we see and read: we're involved in creating shared meaning in our societies. Researchers Heather Mendick, Kim Allen, Laura Harvey and Aisha Ahmad talked to young people in England about their aspirations in the context of austerity. They explored how ideas about class, gender and race are represented in celebrity culture, and how young people make sense of these in relation to their own lives. Through celebrity culture, young people take up, resist or rework different stories about their lives and futures, such as what "success" or "happiness" look like.

The researchers found that the young people they spoke with were very invested in ideas about hard work and meritocracy, but that these were often evaluated in relation to class, gender and race. White businessmen like Bill Gates were seen as "deserving" their wealth, in contrast to reality celebrities from working-class backgrounds like Katie Price. The researchers saw celebrity culture as both something that regulates what is considered possible but also offers resources for making sense of the world around us.

MEDIA PRODUCTION AND SOCIAL CLASS

Access to the production of media is not equal. The most powerful people in society tend to have greater access to the resources to create media – from big-budget film production to the time and resources to create content online. This has an impact on whose stories are told and how different groups are represented.

EVEN WHEN WORKERS FROM "MINORITY" BACKGROUNDS ENTER THE CULTURAL INDUSTRIES, THEY ARE NOT AFFORDED THE SAME CREATIVE FREEDOM AS THEIR WHITE, MALE, MIDDLE-CLASS COUNTERPARTS. THEY FIND THEIR PRACTICE CONSTRAINED BY THOSE AT THE TOP, WHO SEE PRODUCTIONS ABOUT MARGINALITY OR MINORITY EXPERIENCE AS A RISKY INVESTMENT.

RESEARCHERS DAVE O'BRIEN, KIM ALLEN, SAM FRIEDMAN, ANAMIK SAHA

IT'S A GREAT STORY, BUT I JUST DON'T SEE A BIG MARKET FOR IT.

I KNOW LOADS OF PEOPLE WHO WOULD WATCH—

FILLING ADVERTISING SLOTS WOULD BE A REAL CHALLENGE.

The development of digital technologies for media production has made it cheaper and more accessible for many to produce and distribute music, film, audio and writing. This has enabled space for more diverse production and representation, including on corporate platforms like YouTube.

MAKING CLASS THROUGH SOCIAL MEDIA

Many of the ideas we have discussed so far in the book, around class relations, identities, representations and consciousness, can be seen by looking at social media. Technology, the creation and management of content, minerals and energy are all part of global relations of production and representation.

Social media can offer a space for community and self-published content – offering possibilities for more democratic communication and sharing of knowledge and experiences.

CLASS AND SOCIAL MEDIA PRODUCTION

Social media platforms are also profit-making industries. Social class is created through many different kinds of production via social media - from users making sense of their identities by posting and commenting, to relations of exploitation in the production of phones and the "outsourcing" of moderation of offensive content.

BLURRING BOUNDARIES – CULTURAL OMNIVORES

Those in high social positions increasingly act as **cultural omnivores**, consuming both highbrow and lowbrow culture. In some ways, this could be seen as a blurring of traditional class distinctions. However, this does not mean that popular culture is now valued as equal to elite forms of culture. Rather, lowbrow culture must be engaged with in a "knowing" way. Sociologist Mike Savage calls this practice "**emerging cultural capital**", where the middle class consume both the "right" kind of popular culture and the "wrong" kind but in the "right" way.

For example, sociologists Nihal Simay Yalvaç and Irmak Karademir Hazir explored the cooking and eating tastes of middle-class people in Turkey. They found that people who went to more "lowbrow" places to eat still characterized the food as "low status" and performed class distinctions in the way that they talked about the food, places and other people who ate there.

EMERGING CULTURAL CAPITAL IS A PARTICULAR AESTHETIC APPRECIATION, A CERTAIN DETACHED, KNOWING ORIENTATION TO POPULAR CULTURE THAT DEMONSTRATES BOTH AN ECLECTIC KNOWLEDGE AND A PRIVILEGED UNDERSTANDING.

MIKE SAVAGE

YOU JUST HAVE TO LISTEN TO THIS ON VINYL; IT GIVES YOU A MORE AUTHENTIC LISTENING EXPERIENCE.

CULTURAL APPROPRIATION

"Appropriation" refers to taking from a culture that is not your own. This can be culturally specific knowledge, practices or artefacts. Beverley Skeggs uses the idea of prosthetics to talk about how the middle class are able to attach and detach cultural markers to their body in order to extract value from other cultures. Skeggs argues that elements of Black cultures are extracted and made available for the White market, such as music and fashion. By consuming this culture, the White audience is able to take on the values and feelings associated with Black cultures, such as "cool". However, the value depends on which body it is attached to. The separation of "cool" from "dangerous" only works when applied to White bodies; racist systems of thought symbolically connect "cool" and "dangerous" together when applied to Black bodies.

Some writers have questioned whether the concept of "appropriation" reinforces the idea that cultures are inherently separate, or that there is some essential character to them. As we'll see on pages 122-4, the cultural theorist Paul Gilroy has critically analyzed the commodification of difference. However, he also challenges the idea that culture is fixed, pure or owned, tracing histories of Black cultural forms and exploring processes of mixing and cultural exchange.

This process of middle-class appropriation can be seen in the "nu-lad" fashion trend in Britain, where working-class clothing from the 1990s is worn by the middle class today. By putting on the clothes associated with the working class, the middle class gain values of authenticity and cool. But this bourgeois desire to access the value of the working class is often challenged or exposed because it hasn't been acquired through the right experiences.

CHAPTER 6: EVERYDAY

WHY EVERYDAY LIFE MATTERS

Sociologist C. Wright Mills (1916-62) famously called for us to connect our personal troubles to public issues. A focus on everyday life enables us to make this connection. Rather than seeing class as a static structure, an exploration of everyday life reveals class as an emerging identity. By paying attention to everyday life we can understand how class is made and how classed lives unfold in real time and through time.

FOCUSING ON EVERYDAY LIFE MAKES US TAKE THE MUNDANE SERIOUSLY AND ASK WHAT IS AT STAKE IN OUR DAILY ENCOUNTERS WITH NEIGHBOURS OR THE PEOPLE WE BRUSH PAST AT THE BUS STOP.

SOCIOLOGIST LES BACK

In this chapter we will look at how different theorists have explored the role of "the everyday" in the formation and lived experience of class inequality.

PEOPLE AND PLACE

Everyday life is often understood as the backdrop upon which social life plays out. By bringing it into the foreground, we can draw attention to the ways in which patterns of behaviour emerge. A focus on everyday life, on small acts in local places, helps us to connect people and place. Within this framework, people and place are co-constructed – they are made in relation to each other.

115

COMMUNITY

Community is an important way in which people understand their place in the world, both socially and geographically. It is an idea drawn upon by the public, media, politicians and academics to articulate shared identity. However, community is a paradoxical idea. On the one hand, community is an act of inclusion, based on assumptions of sameness and unity. On the other, this very act of inclusion requires the exclusion of those defined as different and outside of the community.

Therefore, our interest in community is to question how community is made. When is community claimed and by who? Who is included in this claim and who is excluded?

MAKING COMMUNITY

> HOWEVER MUCH WE MAY WANT IT, COMMUNITY NEVER SEEMS TO ARRIVE.
>
> YOUTH WORKER JEREMY BRENT
> (1950–2006)

Community is often critiqued for being "imagined" and impossible to realize. However, illusions are very much part of social and political life and, therefore, community has real effects.

Community often evokes feelings of comfort and stability associated with a time gone by. However, it is not static: it is all about movement and change. Community is always made in dialogue with fantasy, as people recreate, reject or transform narratives of what community means.

THE COMMUNITY CENTRE

Community centres or community halls are public places where members of the community come together for activities, social support and information. They can be established by grassroots community organizations, the government, sponsored as a charity or run on a commercial basis.

Although community centres may seem an obvious place to look for community, they are highly contested sites. They are a place where the community encounters the state and other powerful organizations. From the design of the building to the funding of activities, the community centre encapsulates the tension between structure and agency in everyday life.

CUTS TO THE COMMUNITY

Human geographer John Horton's research explores how austerity has tangible effects on the everyday running of community centres. He argues the anticipation of funding cuts creates an atmosphere where anxieties about, and hopes for, young people's futures become intensified. The anticipation of funding cuts has everyday, lived consequences that are arguably more wide-ranging, intractable and troubling than the impacts of funding cuts themselves. Young people experiencing cuts to services come to see themselves and their area as not worth investing in. While this can lead to feelings of shame, it is often accompanied by a rejection of negative stereotypes and a sense of pride in the local community.

DEVALUED IDENTITIES

Working-class people must negotiate their position of social disadvantage, using a range of cultural performances to generate value for themselves, among their peers and within their community.

Investing in appearance, clothes and jewellery is one way the working class develop a positive image of themselves. However, these cultural styles are often devalued within dominant middle-class culture.

Les Back's research looks at the meanings that working-class people attach to their appearance and the way tattoos, jewellery and style are a central part of expressing individual, kinship and community identities.

EACH OF THE ITEMS WORN CARRIES A MEANING AND ASSOCIATION THAT ESCAPES THE STRICTURES OF BOURGEOIS IGNORANCE AND PREJUDICE. EACH SYMBOLIZES A MOMENT PASSED IN LIVING, A REGISTER OF LOVE OR KINSHIP, OR TO THE MEMORY OF THE LOST.

LES BACK

HYBRID IDENTITIES

Classed culture is not fixed; it is made through the weaving together of different identities. Hybrid identities are created when cultural styles from across the world come together.

Global, cross-cultural interactions are central to the formation of many youth cultures around the world. Mass communication and what sociologist Manuel Castells calls the "network society" are spaces in which ideas and music can travel.

Different cultural styles can be embodied through the consumption of music, fashion and ways of talking.

GRIME MUSIC IN THE UK EXPRESSES EVERYDAY EXPERIENCES, FROM CLASS, GENDER AND ETHNIC CONFLICTS AND FINANCIAL HARDSHIPS, TO PLEASURE, FRIENDSHIP AND GOOD TIMES.

MEDIA AND COMMUNICATION RESEARCHER LEE BARRON

MULTICULTURALISM

"Multiculturalism" is often used to describe mixed ethnic communities, but it is also a set of values, policies and practices which inform how such communities are created and understood.

Multiculturalism is located within both national and international contexts. Its foundations are based on the moral and political ideals of the post-World War II settlement, while also being tied to global issues such as migration, settlement and rights.

Philosopher Will Kymlicka has explored the development of multicultural policies in Western democracies.

FROM THE 1960S, POLICIES AIMED AT "MULTICULTURAL CITIZENSHIP" FOCUSED ON ISSUES SUCH AS RECOGNITION AND RIGHTS FOR INDIGENOUS COMMUNITIES, DIFFERENT LEVELS OF AUTONOMY FOR NATIONAL GROUPS WITHIN STATES (SUCH AS BASQUES AND CATALANS IN SPAIN), AND FUNDING AND SUPPORT FOR MULTICULTURAL EDUCATION AND ACTIVITIES.

WILL KYMLICKA

Paul Gilroy has pointed to the diverse ways that the idea of multiculturalism has been taken up in different contexts – it does not always mean the same thing. Government policies, equal opportunities initiatives, local community events and commercial representations of difference have all been framed in relation to multiculturalism.

There was a strong "backlash" against multiculturalism in the USA and UK in the 1980s and 90s, as right-wing critiques of affirmative action and anti-racism became dominant.

These ideas continue today, in speeches by politicians about White working-class young people being "left behind" or excluded by multicultural education. Sociologist Anoop Nayak's research argues that some White working-class youth may feel that they are "victims" of modern day anti-racism.

123

CONVIVIALITY

> I HOPE THAT AN INTEREST IN THE WORKINGS OF CONVIVIALITY WILL TAKE OFF FROM WHERE "MULTICULTURALISM" BROKE DOWN.

PAUL GILROY

Paul Gilroy argues that multiculture is an everyday feature of social life in postcolonial cities. He suggests that we should look to these urban spaces as sites of conviviality, where people live and interact across social and cultural differences. Gilroy is pointing to something more complex than distinct cultures interacting. Conviviality describes cultural interdependence – in which different habits and experiences flow and inform each other as people live side by side. This does not mean that racism no longer exists, but suggests that we can understand how class, ethnic and gender differences are created by looking at everyday interactions.

SOCIAL MIX OR SOCIAL MIXING

"Social mix" refers to the make-up of a place based on indicators of difference, for example ethnicity, class and gender. Social mixing is the interactions between people across these differences, for example in friendships.

A "good social mix" is celebrated because it aims to redistribute opportunities across social inequalities. However, research by Sumi Hollingworth and Ayo Mansaray found that social mixing in schools often reproduced existing social hierarchies and inequalities.

THE CAFETERIA IS ALL BLACK PEOPLE AND THEN OUTSIDE ALL THE WHITE PEOPLE GO ON THE VERANDA TRYING TO SUNBATHE AND STUFF.

Wendy Bottero explains that social mixing is prevented by a process of "differential association", where the connections we feel to others are not a personal preference but based on sharing similar social resources.

THE HIDDEN INJURIES OF CLASS

Living in a classed society has emotional costs across class divides. Well-being measures indicate that the most unequal societies are the unhappiest. Inequality does not feel good for the rich or the poor. Social epidemiologists Richard Wilkinson and Kate Pickett explain that as the gap between the rich and the poor widens, status insecurity increases, heightening anxiety. The widespread belief in meritocracy means that any failure is seen as a personal failure, resulting in feelings of shame.

NOT ONLY HAVE MEASURES OF WELL-BEING AND HAPPINESS CEASED TO RISE WITH ECONOMIC GROWTH BUT, AS AFFLUENT SOCIETIES HAVE GROWN RICHER, THERE HAVE BEEN LONG-TERM RISES IN RATES OF ANXIETY, DEPRESSION AND NUMEROUS OTHER SOCIAL PROBLEMS.

RICHARD WILKINSON AND KATE PICKETT

126

PSYCHOSOCIAL

As we saw earlier, scholars like Frantz Fanon and Valerie Walkerdine have pointed to the links between psychological and social aspects of class. The social psychologist Helen Lucey argues that this psychosocial approach challenges the traditional separation of the internal psyche and the external world, suggesting that psychological and social processes are connected. Lucey's research explores how narratives of sisters provide a unique insight into how sameness and difference shape our sense of self.

Sisters are connected to each other and to previous generations in material ways (such as inherited physical and personality traits and wealth) and in social ways (such as likes and dislikes, expectations and desires). Sisters' stories can show us how class is experienced by revealing the ways in which we walk the fine identity line of being a unique individual as well as part of a group.

CLASS AND EMOTION

> CLASS IS SOMETHING BENEATH YOUR CLOTHES, UNDER YOUR SKIN, IN YOUR REFLEXES, IN YOUR PSYCHE, AT THE VERY CORE OF YOUR BEING.

CULTURAL HISTORIAN ANNETTE KUHN

For the working class, being positioned as inferior can be felt in everyday interactions, where a look or comment can mark you out as "other".

The working class's emotional responses to inequality are often pathologized as psychologically abnormal; however, we can see them as legitimate reactions to encountering unfairness on a daily basis. So emotions such as anger and envy are the result of an unequal society.

> THESE TABLETS WILL HELP YOU TO FEEL LESS STRESSED.

> BUT THEY WONT HELP ME FIND WORK AND PAY MY RENT!

Sociologist Yusef Bakkali argues that the lives of marginalized young adults are defined by the psychosocial experience of "**munpain**" – where pain has become a mundane part of their everyday life.

SOCIAL MOBILITY AND SHAME

Because classed differences become embodied, they are carried with you throughout your life. So even when someone from a working-class background achieves social mobility, they often have to self-consciously censor their behaviour so that their classed origin doesn't slip out.

Education scholar Valerie Hey reflects on her own trajectory from a Northern working-class community to a Southern elite university in the UK, where her Northern accent positions her in the "wrong class" as soon as she speaks.

IN A CLASS SOCIETY, YOU CAN "FEEL IN THE WRONG" OR BE PUT THERE WHEN YOU LITERALLY OPEN YOUR MOUTH. WITHIN THE CONTEXT OF UK HIGHER EDUCATION, HAVING THE RIGHT "ACCENT" CONTINUES TO MARK DISTINCTION, "PLACING" YOU IN THE EDUCATED/UNEDUCATED CLASSES.

VALERIE HEY

EMPLOYEES ONLY!

I WORK HERE!

MIDDLE-CLASS GUILT

The middle class can experience difficult emotions when reconciling their relative privilege with ideas of fairness and equality of opportunity. This emotional work is often gendered, with middle-class women carrying the burden of managing relationships with domestic workers, balancing work and care commitments, and living up to the ideal of responsible consumption.

Emotions arising from positions of privilege, such as guilt, can be a motivating factor in producing social change. However, these emotions can also reinforce classed divisions of "us" and "them". For example, human geographer Abby Hickcox's research showed that White middle-class environmentalists in the USA considered poor immigrant and non-immigrant Latinx as unaware, uninterested or unable to participate in environmentalism - furthering class and racial exclusion.

LIVABLE LIFE

For philosopher Judith Butler, a "livable life" is an important part of being human; this means that you experience life beyond simply surviving.

In order for a life to be livable, it must be perceptible: others must recognize your life as of value.

Therefore, although it is important to document inequality, it is also important to acknowledge the ways in which the working class live their lives. If working-class culture is to be valued in society, then both media and academic representations of the working class need to explore examples of everyday joy, humour and community. This will help develop a broader understanding of how working-class people can experience a life in which they thrive.

FRIENDSHIPS

Friendships are an intimate form of social relationships, often understood as founded on individual choice and personal preference. Yet, despite this apparent freedom, friendships tend to be patterned in terms of social class and ethnicity.

THIS PROCESS IS CALLED "HOMOPHILY", WHERE PEOPLE'S RELATIONSHIPS ARE BASED ON THEIR SIMILARITIES, AS EXPRESSED IN THE SAYING THAT "BIRDS OF A FEATHER FLOCK TOGETHER".

Feminists have long argued that we need to explore the role of power in the "private" domain. This raises the question of how our individual experiences (feelings, subjectivities, emotions, memories) are related to dominant and systematic features of social life.

Friendships can be understood as a social practice which enables the sharing of resources. As some social groups have access to more economic, social and cultural resources than others, this means that friendships among the elite facilitate access to resources and help to reproduce class privilege.

ALL SOCIAL NETWORKS GENERATE RELATIONSHIPS OF MUTUALITY, TRUST AND CO-OPERATION. WHAT VARY ARE THE TYPES AND QUALITY OF RESOURCES AVAILABLE THROUGH EXCHANGES OF MUTUALITY.

SOCIOLOGIST PATRICIA FERNÁNDEZ-KELLY

MY SON IS INTERESTED IN GETTING SOME WORK EXPERIENCE.

NO PROBLEM, HE CAN START ON MONDAY.

GIFT-GIVING

Gift-giving in the form of food or other "essentials" is a common practice within poorer communities. However, because of a discomfort with ideas of "charity" and the negative stereotypes associated with being in "need", this form of gift-giving is often a veiled practice.

The gift-giver must take on the emotional work of repositioning the gift as a burden which the recipient may relieve them of through acceptance of the gift. This performance undermines traditional constructions of the gift as reciprocal; in everyday gift-giving there is an insistence that the gift need not be reciprocated. There is a necessity and urgency attached to the everyday gift that separates it from the more indulgent gifts of festivals and birthdays.

Gift-giving within working-class communities demonstrates how material inequalities are mediated through cultural practices that resist, subvert and reform meanings.

CHAPTER 7: THEMES AND DEBATES

As a lived experience, mode of economic organization and academic inquiry, the issue of class does not remain static. Class is a "live" issue and contemporary thinkers continue to challenge the assumptions underpinning the "classic" theories of class. In this chapter, we explore current themes and debates in the study of class: the role that ideas of class play in politics; the intersections of class, gender, race and disability; and the impact of class in shaping our minds and bodies.

THE DEATH OF CLASS?

The 1990s saw claims across Western academia and politics that traditional categorizations of class were breaking down.

CLASS HAS COLLAPSED AND IS DECOMPOSING, LEAVING ONLY THE MEREST TRACES OF ITS EFFECTS.

The Death of Class

Jan Pakulski
Malcolm Waters

Sociologist Ulrich Beck (1944–2015) was a key proponent of this critique, suggesting that Western societies had entered a new phase of modernity in which the categories and assumptions of the past had been torn apart. Beck argued that it was the processes of modernity itself, such as new technologies and new knowledge, that had produced the next stage of reflexive modernity.

According to Beck, conflicts in society are no longer defined by the social production and distribution of *wealth*, but the production and distribution of *risk*. Class interests have been replaced by the threat of new global risks which dissolve old boundaries and unite all victims of risk.

WE ALL NEED TO GET TO SAFETY.

Individuals are removed from traditional roles and re-embedded in ones where they must construct their own biographies and self identities. Reflexive decision-making is central to identity formation as individuals search for self-fulfillment through consumption.

THE THIRD WAY

The connection between social change and academic theorizations of this change is most clearly demonstrated in the rise of "Third Way" politics. Informed by British sociologist Anthony Giddens, Third Way politics is founded upon the idea that class-based divisions of left and right are redundant.

Giddens argued that traditional Labour voters from blue-collar working-class backgrounds were disappearing due to three key transformations in modern society: globalization, the knowledge economy and individualization. Therefore, he suggested that left-leaning political parties should generate consensual support by campaigning from the centre.

We can see how Third Way politics was directly informed by debates surrounding the "breakdown" of class and the rise of individualism. For example, the Third Way aimed to reform government to be transparent and customer-oriented; called for the construction of a new social contract which connected rights and responsibilities; highlighted the importance of personal development through lifelong learning; and sought to tackle emerging risks of "welfare dependency", crime and global warming.

PRODUCTION VS CONSUMPTION

Sociologist Zygmunt Bauman (1925–2017) argued that we have moved from a society of producers to a society of consumers. Our consumption practices are the key principle of social inclusion and exclusion, guiding the distribution of social esteem and stigma. We have begun to view consumption as a universal human right and duty. Class and gender inequalities are ignored, as consumerist performance becomes the new mode of stratification. The most disturbing feature of the consumer society, Bauman argues, is that the pressure to transform your subjectivity through consumption is driven by the need to become a marketable commodity yourself.

THE SOCIETY OF CONSUMERS DOES NOT RECOGNIZE DIFFERENCES OF AGE OR GENDER (HOWEVER COUNTERFACTUALLY) AND WILL NOT MAKE ALLOWANCES FOR EITHER; NOR DOES IT (BLATANTLY COUNTERFACTUALLY) RECOGNIZE CLASS DISTINCTIONS.

ZYGMUNT BAUMAN

Sociologist Antonio Cambra González's research into the electro dance scene in France showed how dancers used self-commodification to further their career. Becoming a celebrity required dancers to display their identity on social media as a brand. However, social media does not necessarily democratize the formation of celebrity, as middle-class resources such as access to technical equipment and cultural knowledge helped dancers to succeed. Moreover, dance styles that emerge from more diverse scenes are stripped of class, sexual or ethnic meanings in order to become attractive for the middle-class consumer audience.

wild_winter_dancer

Follow

542 likes

wild_winter_dancer 'It's the most wonderful time of the year' 😊 ❤

#Humble #grafter #blessed #grateful #nofilter #cleaneating #livingbestlife #kale smoothie

CULTURAL VS MATERIAL ANALYSIS OF CLASS

Theorists continue to debate whether class analysis should focus on material inequalities emerging from market processes or cultural differences founded on consumption and lifestyle.

The "**cultural turn**" in class analysis developed in response to the centrality of economics in measurements of class. Sociologists Fiona Devine and Mike Savage argue that class inequality is routinely reproduced through both economic and social practices. So, rather than assuming your economic position determines your cultural dispositions, we need to consider how the two are interconnected. Research in this tradition explores the lived experience of class formation, questioning the role of culture and lifestyle in modes of exclusion and domination.

ALTHOUGH THEIR CLOTHES ARE VALUED BY THEIR PEERS, THEY ARE ALSO SEEN AS A SIGN OF DEVIANCE BY THE POLICE.

CULTURE

Alongside the "cultural turn" there has been a "return" to a **material** understanding of class through a political economy lens. This approach aims to map the connections between society, politics and the economy. It foregrounds the role of the relations of production, political institutions and ideologies in the formation of class. This work ranges from broad analysis of the economic structures of capitalism to smaller-scale research on the impact of the market on people's lives.

COLLECTIVITY VS DIFFERENTIATION

There has been a shift in class analysis from "old" accounts of class as categorical, explicit and collective to "new" theorizations of class as relational, tacit and hierarchical. Although individualization has weakened collective class identities, people still define their identity through processes of differentiation between class cultures.

Wendy Bottero argues that there is a problematic slippage between these "old" and "new" understandings of class. She suggests that "new" understandings of class need to break away from "old" class categories. So, rather than talking about class, we need to talk about **hierarchy**. For Bottero, class refers to social identity and division founded upon economic conditions. Hierarchies, on the other hand, are individualized distinctions, reproduced in our everyday practices, that position us in relation to each other. She believes that inequality is difficult to eradicate because it is generated through our most banal and mundane activities.

CLASS CONDITIONS VS CLASS PERCEPTIONS

Contemporary class theorists note a disconnect between class conditions and subjective perceptions of these conditions. The sociologist John Scott acknowledges that critics of class analysis are right to suggest that class differences are now less directly reflected in our attitudes and outlook. However, class relations continue to exist and impact our conditions of life. Therefore, we must recognize the interplay between class and other lines of social division in the formation of social identities.

Beverley Skeggs calls the rejection of class identity "dis-identification". She argues that the pathologization of the working class means that people don't want to claim this identity because it is devalued. Her research found that working-class women rejected a working-class identity in order to be seen as respectable. Therefore, the denial of class is the result of class processes.

CLASS PERCEPTIONS IN SOCIAL RESEARCH

The valuing of a class match between researcher and participant is an assumption underpinning much social research on class. Sharing a class identity with your participant is seen to help you build rapport and produce a more respectful research interaction. However, this assumes that identity is one-dimensional and fixed. Reflections from researchers highlight the complexity and intersections of class identities; we may find that participants reject the class identities applied to them, or they do not recognize the researcher's claim to a particular class identity.

Sociologists Jody Mellor, Nicola Ingram, Jessie Abrahams and Phoebe Beedell argue that we need to move beyond attempts to class-match the researcher and participant and instead explore **positionality** in our research. By reflecting on the power dynamics of the research interaction, we can understand the significance of the subjective experiences and material realities of class for the researcher and participant in the production of knowledge about class.

STRUCTURAL VS POSTSTRUCTURAL

Class has traditionally been understood from a structural perspective. Structural accounts foreground the role of determining factors, such as occupation, housing and education. This perspective suggests that our class position is a consequence of material differences.

Post-structural approaches explore the processes through which class is made, rather than determined, which means they allow us to consider how class categories are subverted. Although post-structural theory has been critiqued for moving away from the material foundation of inequalities, through a focus on language, the deconstruction of class categories is not the same as rejecting the material inequalities of class. Many contemporary class theorists have turned to post-structural theory as a way to critically engage with the role class categories play in the reproduction of inequality.

MUM WORKS IN CARE + COUNCIL FLAT + STATE SCHOOL = WORKING CLASS

- feminist values
- poor pay
- empathy & inclusive practices

- diverse cultures
- affordable housing
- stigma

- underfunded
- peer pressure
- favourite subject

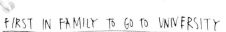

= FIRST IN FAMILY TO GO TO UNIVERSITY
= CREATIVE (ART, MUSIC, ACTING)
= COMMUNITY LEADER

143

IDENTITY VS IDENTIFICATION

Cultural theorist Stuart Hall suggested there are two distinct ways of thinking about identity. The first approach assumes that identity is intrinsic or essential to people who share a common origin or structural experience. For instance, if you share a material position such as being born into a family with a similar occupation, housing and education, you will share a similar identity, the same likes and dislikes.

The second approach understands identity as a matter of "becoming" rather than "being". Scholars from this perspective argue that an authentic identity based on shared origins does not exist. Instead, identity is understood as relational and always incomplete, in the process of making through the differences drawn with other identities.

Hall developed the concept of **identification** to capture the way identity is never singular and unified, but constructed across different discourses, practices and positions.

> IDENTIFICATION IS A PROCESS OF MAKING THE SELF BY DRAWING SYMBOLIC BOUNDARIES. THESE BOUNDARIES ARE PRODUCED THROUGH OUR WAYS OF TALKING AND ACTING; THEY CREATE LINES OF INCLUSION AND EXCLUSION, "US" AND "THEM". IDENTIFICATION REQUIRES SOMETHING OR SOMEONE TO BE LEFT OUTSIDE. WHAT IS LEFT OUTSIDE IS AS MUCH PART OF THE IDENTITY AS WHAT IS INSIDE; IN THIS WAY IT IS A CONSTITUTIVE OUTSIDE.

STUART HALL

CLASS AND THE BODY

Categorizations such as class come alive through repetitive embodied acts. The making of class identity involves a dual process whereby the body is physically transformed and meanings are attached to these socially produced differences. This process of making class through marking bodies is called **inscription**.

> INSCRIPTION REFERS TO THE WAY THAT VALUE IS TRANSFERRED ONTO BODIES AND READ OFF THEM, AND THE MECHANISMS BY WHICH IT IS RETAINED, ACCUMULATED, LOST OR APPROPRIATED.

BEVERLEY SKEGGS

The shaping of our body by our social position has emotional consequences. Pierre Bourdieu's research in a rural community in France highlighted that farmers were embarrassed by their bodies, which they felt bore traces of their low social standing. Bourdieu suggested that the farmers internalized the judgements of others and started to see themselves as "peasants". The farmers developed an "unhappy consciousness" of how their body was viewed by others, which in turn fed into their behaviour.

INTERSECTIONALITY

Kimberlé Crenshaw argues that we need to account for the multiple dimensions of identity in order to understand how oppression is experienced. She developed the theory of intersectionality to understand the structural, political and representational aspects of the experiences of women of colour.

Structural intersectionality refers to how the burdens that result from class and gender oppressions are exacerbated by racial discrimination. When support for women of colour is founded upon the experiences of women from different race or class backgrounds, it creates a further dimension of disempowerment because it does not account for the specific obstacles emerging from intersecting oppressions.

Women of colour are positioned by multiple oppressions, but they face the fragmentation of their identity when feminist and anti-racist groups pursue conflicting political agendas. Not only do these groups fail to account for the "additional" oppressions experienced by women of colour, they often lack a full understanding of the specific ways women of colour experience sexism and racism. This is **political intersectionality**.

Representational intersectionality refers to how the representation of women of colour in popular media can also be a source of disempowerment. Beliefs about women of colour are built and maintained by how they are represented, misrepresented, or not represented in the media. Both the production of images of women of colour and critiques of these images that only focus on "race" or "gender" ignore the mutual reinforcement of racial and sexual subordination.

THE IDEA OF THE "UNDERCLASS"

In his history of the "underclass" idea, John Welshman argues that the differentiation between poor people deemed "deserving" and those who are deemed "undeserving" has been a dominant theme in UK social policy since the 1880s. He suggests that various "underclass" labels and theories have been used to demonize, control and punish the poor across history.

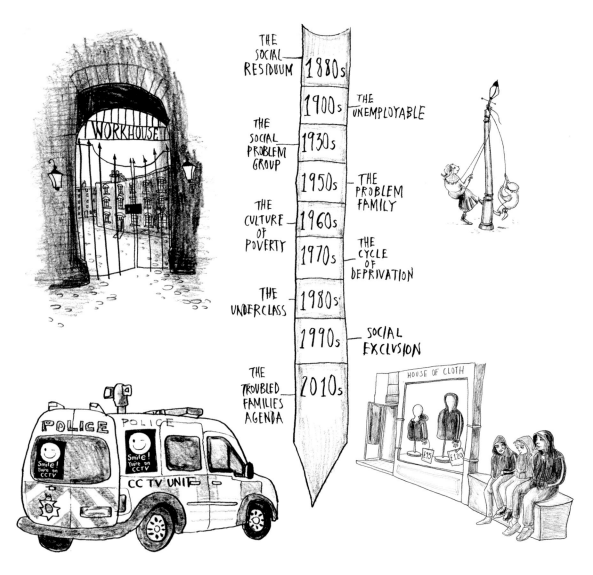

THE SOCIAL RESIDUUM — 1880s

1900s — THE UNEMPLOYABLE

THE SOCIAL PROBLEM GROUP — 1930s

1950s — THE PROBLEM FAMILY

THE CULTURE OF POVERTY — 1960s

1970s — THE CYCLE OF DEPRIVATION

THE UNDERCLASS — 1980s

1990s — SOCIAL EXCLUSION

THE TROUBLED FAMILIES AGENDA — 2010s

WORKHOUSE

POLICE · POLICE · Smile! You're on CCTV · CC TV UNIT

HOUSE OF CLOTH · £15 · £20

Sociologist Tracy Shildrick's research with families facing worklessness and social deprivation found that the "Troubled Families Programme" (UK, 2015–20) reflected "underclass" ideas by focusing on the supposed moral and behavioural deficits of families rather than the structural causes of poverty and disadvantage. The stigmatizing label of "troubled families" is used to develop public consent for punitive social policies.

DISABILITY AND CLASS

The social model of disability highlights how people are disabled by the barriers they face in society, rather than by their impairment or difference. Barriers can be physical, for example the accessibility of buildings, or based on values and beliefs, such as assumptions that disabled people cannot do certain things.

Chris Grover and Linda Piggott offer a Marxist analysis of disability. They argue that there is a tension within the social model of disability, where the disadvantages of disabled people are addressed through removing barriers to work, without acknowledging the exploitative and disabling nature of wage labour.

Grover and Piggott argue that the British government uses "the right to work" to drive authoritarian and disabling welfare reforms which increasingly link benefit receipt to the pursuit of waged labour. In order to disrupt the way paid work has been viewed as the only way for people to demonstrate their citizenship responsibilities, we need to make a case for the "right not to work".

THE RIGHT NOT TO WORK IS THE RIGHT NOT TO HAVE YOUR VALUE DETERMINED BY YOUR PRODUCTIVITY AS A WORKER, BY YOUR EMPLOYABILITY OR SALARY … IT IS ABOUT CULTIVATING A SKEPTICAL ATTITUDE REGARDING THE SIGNIFICANCE OF WORK, WHICH SHOULD NOT BE TAKEN AT FACE VALUE AS A SIGN OF EQUALITY AND ENFRANCHISEMENT, BUT SHOULD BE ANALYZED MORE CRITICALLY.

ARTIST AND DISABILITY ACTIVIST SUNNY TAYLOR

Disability is therefore contested, with moral distinctions made between what does and does not count as a disability. Classed processes play into this, with welfare payments for disabled people becoming a site of judgement over the deserving or undeserving character of the individual, rather than acknowledging the barriers facing the day-to-day lives of people with disabilities.

CLASS AND RACISM

Sociologist Satnam Virdee argues that we must situate racism within a historical analysis of capitalism. He suggests that capitalism is inherently unstable and, to be maintained, requires the production of social differences of race, nation and geographical origins. Racialized differentiation creates new hierarchies within the working class, enabling some to achieve an enhanced status, while others are further exploited. The structural and symbolic stratification of the working class prevents the development of class consciousness.

This process was apparent in much of the Trump and Brexit campaigns, whereby nationalist populism recast the injuries of class (felt by all within the same socio-economic group) through racialized identity politics (as injuries felt exclusively by White workers because of socially inclusive government policies).

Nevertheless, Virdee points to everyday multiculture as a source of hope and a basis for an alternative class politics. As the sociologist Sivamohan Valluvan notes, our understanding of class inequality must remain attentive to migrant and minority subjects. He points to communities where an "indifference to difference" is the norm as a site where everyday practices offer new forms of collective identity and action.

The activism that followed the tragic Grenfell Tower fire in London in 2017, where 72 people lost their lives, foregrounded the intersection of ethnicity, citizenship status and class in the neglect experienced by working-class communities. The residents had raised concerns about fire safety many times before the fire. Cladding on the side of the building had enabled the fire to spread quickly. The former residents of Grenfell Tower and members of the local community are campaigning for justice.

CHAPTER 8: THE FUTURE OF CLASS

Throughout the book, we have tried to point to both the processes involved in the creation and experiences of class, and actions that people have taken in response to class inequality. In this chapter, we'll look at some different strategies that groups are using to resist and organize around class inequality.

AS SOON AS THERE IS A POWER RELATION, THERE IS THE POSSIBILITY OF RESISTANCE.

PHILOSOPHER MICHEL FOUCAULT

IT SEEMS LIKE THERE IS SO MUCH IN SOCIETY THAT CREATES AND REINFORCES CLASS INEQUALITY. MAKES ME FEEL LIKE IT'S IMPOSSIBLE TO DO ANYTHING ABOUT IT!

THERE ARE SO MANY PEOPLE AND GROUPS RESISTING CLASS INEQUALITY.

WE'LL SHOW YOU DIFFERENT STRATEGIES PEOPLE HAVE USED, AND HOPEFULLY INSPIRE YOU TO TAKE ACTION.

Sociologists Anna Johansson and Stellan Vinthagen highlight the importance of everyday resistance. They argue that everyday resistance can take the form of routine acts that are not often detected as resistance because they are not formally organized. Everyday resistance grows out of the social conditions and life experience of the people who do the resisting. Therefore, methods of resistance often include using the systems of power that resistors are struggling against.

PREFIGURATIVE POLITICS

The concept of "prefigurative politics" was put forward by social scientist Carl Boggs in 1977. The idea has been used by academics and activists to describe social movements which try to enact the forms of social relations they wish to see in wider society.

For example, during the Egyptian Revolution in 2011, Tahrir Square became a site of political discussion, collective resistance and food distribution. Political scientist Mariz Tadros explored the emergence of youth-led groups in the square, who took action to counter sexual violence against women during the uprising. Tadros sees this as a form of prefigurative politics – acting in the "here and now" rather than calling for change in the future.

Social policy researchers Armine Ishkanian and Anita Peña Saavedra point to another example in the UK. Sisters Uncut is a feminist group founded in 2014, who oppose the UK government's spending cuts to services for the victims of domestic violence. They argue that individual experiences of domestic violence are shaped by interconnected systems of oppression such as racism, sexism, classism and disablism. So, for Sisters Uncut, prefiguration means translating their commitment to intersectionality into practice.

WE NEED TO CHALLENGE AND ADDRESS HARMFUL BEHAVIOUR, SYSTEMS AND RELATIONSHIPS. WHEN SOMEONE EXPERIENCES HARM WITHIN SISTERS UNCUT, WE LOOK TO THE VALUES, BEHAVIOURS AND POWER DYNAMICS OF THE WHOLE GROUP FOR ANSWERS ABOUT HOW THIS HAPPENED AND HOW WE CAN TRANSFORM OUR PRACTICE.

NUISANCE AS RESISTANCE

Performance and cultural politics academic Lynne McCarthy has explored what happens when "private" struggles, such as those over housing inequality and eviction, are brought into the public sphere through collective action in the form of troublemaking or "nuisance".

In London, the Focus E15 campaign began in 2013 after a group of young mothers living in a homeless shelter were served eviction notices. Due to cuts in housing benefit and the lack of affordable housing in London, the women faced being moved to other cities in the UK. They organized protests and occupied disused social housing, drawing attention to the consequences of viewing property in terms of profit rather than as homes.

The women struggled to get their concerns heard by the local council and so used loudspeakers at public events to confront those in power. McCarthy argues that making public vocal claims is a feminist strategy of resistance. The women were seen as out of place in the public political sphere and were removed from the Town Hall and the Town Fair. However, they used this nuisance as a strategy of their protest, drawing attention to their fight against displacement. The mothers' demands were met and they were rehoused in the local area; their campaign continues to fight for decent housing for all.

CLASS ORGANIZATION

A trade union is an organization of workers who aim to maintain or improve their employment conditions. They are often funded through membership fees, and their elected leaders negotiate with employers on behalf of all members.

For example, garment workers across the Global South have been particularly vulnerable to the health and economic impacts of Covid-19. Millions are struggling to survive, as fashion companies refuse to pay their wages in the context of reduced sales. Garment workers' unions are campaigning globally for wages to be paid and safer working conditions.

Trade unions also work with other groups to campaign for change – for example, garment unions collaborating with the Clean Clothes Campaign to put pressure on fashion brands to pay their workers.

Employment Relations researchers Gabriella Alberti and Davide Però argue that in Britain, low-paid and precarious migrant workers are central actors in the renewal of trade union movements through grassroots campaigns. Bigger trade unions do not always meet the needs of precarious workers: translation issues can impact the accessibility of resources and meetings, and outsourced workers face specific issues that aren't always considered by union branches.

RADICAL NOSTALGIA

The word "radical" is formed from the latin word for "root". The social geographer Alastair Bonnett explores the relationship between radicalism and roots, asking whether radicalism requires us to pull up our roots or nurture them. He argues that nostalgia is an important part of our radical imagination. Radical nostalgia – revisiting historical resistance – aims to use the past as a resource for remaking the present.

RADICAL NOSTALGICS DO NOT WANT TO RETURN TO THE PAST, BUT INSTEAD USE IT TO RIGHT HISTORICAL INJUSTICES, BOTH BY HONOURING THOSE WHO WOULD OTHERWISE BE FORGOTTEN AND BY CONTINUING THEIR STRUGGLES.

POLITICAL HISTORIAN EMILY ROBINSON

IN 1915 WE LED A RENT STRIKE IN GLASGOW IN RESPONSE TO THE HIGH RENTS IMPOSED BY PRIVATE LANDLORDS. OVER 20,000 PEOPLE REFUSED TO PAY RENT, PHYSICALLY RESISTED EVICTIONS AND FOUGHT THEM IN COURT. WITHIN MONTHS THE GOVERNMENT PASSED EMERGENCY LEGISLATION TO CONTROL RENT LEVELS.

IN 2021, STUDENTS FROM 45 UNIVERSITIES IN THE UK HELD RENT STRIKES IN RESPONSE TO THE ENFORCEMENT OF COVID-19 CAMPUS LOCKDOWNS, WITH SOME OF US PAYING FOR ROOMS WE COULDN'T RETURN TO AND OTHERS FACING RESTRICTIONS ON THE FACILITIES WE COULD ACCESS.

CLASS DISCRIMINATION

Across the world, there are different laws and policies used to try to address inequalities, for example by making particular forms of discrimination illegal.

In 1958 the International Labour Organization (ILO) created a Convention on Discrimination in employment. States which signed the treaty committed to eliminating discrimination at work, including that based on "social origin", which includes social class, socio-occupational category and caste. Similarly, the European Convention of Human Rights grants protection on the basis of social origin, property, birth or other status.

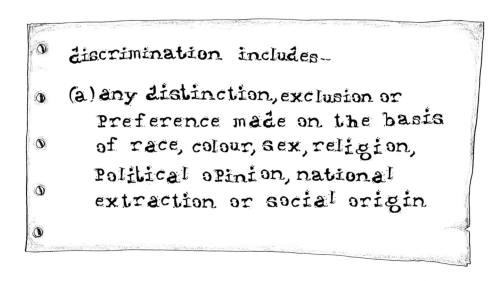

discrimination includes...

(a) any distinction, exclusion or preference made on the basis of race, colour, sex, religion, political opinion, national extraction or social origin

At the national level, governments put in place legislation around discrimination, often using this to put international agreements into national law.

In the UK, the Equality Act 2010 made it unlawful to discriminate against anyone because of:

- age
- gender reassignment
- being married or in a civil partnership
- being pregnant or on maternity leave
- disability
- race, including colour, nationality, ethnic or national origin
- religion or belief
- sex
- sexual orientation.

These aspects of our identity are called "protected characteristics". The state, companies and individuals must ensure that they do not discriminate, harass or victimize people in the UK because of these characteristics. Despite the international commitment to prevent discrimination related to social origin, the UK still does not recognize class as a protected characteristic.

As we have seen throughout the book, social class is a category that can be hard to pin down, which poses challenges for legislation around discrimination.

A 2021 report by the Social Mobility Commission in England argued that socio-economic background (SEB) should be made a protected characteristic. They were looking at discrimination by SEB in the Civil Service. They argued that making this a protected characteristic would help employers to put policies and practices in place to address discrimination.

In 2020 a UK court ruled that the common use of "No DSS" in property rental adverts, which bans tenants who receive welfare benefits, is unlawful. The court found that a ban on tenants who receive state support indirectly discriminates against women and people with disabilities. This could be the first step towards the recognition of class as a protected characteristic.

UNIVERSAL BASIC INCOME

Universal basic income (UBI) is a policy proposal whereby the state provides monthly cash payments to all citizens to enable them to live free from economic insecurity. UBI is equally paid to all members of the community. It is not means-tested and does not require anything in return. This might sound too good to be true, but UBI is growing in popularity and has been trialled in Kenya, Finland, Namibia, India and Canada.

Universal basic income addresses the connected inequalities of race, gender, disability and class. Business and management academics Andrew Johnson and Katherine Roberto argue that in the context of insecure job markets, UBI would help millions out of poverty and increase consumer spending. They point to the uncertainty caused by the global Covid-19 pandemic, and argue that UBI could help provide some certainty for the years ahead.

POVERTY IS NOT THE RESULT OF INDIVIDUAL INABILITY OR IMMORALITY BUT STEMS FROM MARKET FAILURES AND DISCRIMINATORY PRACTICES THAT FORCE PEOPLE INTO UNEMPLOYMENT.

MARTIN LUTHER KING, JR.

FEMINISTS SHOULD ENDORSE A BASIC INCOME BECAUSE IT PROMOTES GENDER EQUALITY BY CREATING THE SOCIAL AND ECONOMIC CONDITIONS REQUIRED TO REDUCE THE GENDERED DIVISION OF LABOUR AND REDUCES THE POVERTY RATE OF THE MOST VULNERABLE GROUP IN CAPITALIST ECONOMIES: SINGLE WOMEN AND THEIR CHILDREN.

POLITICAL SCIENTIST ALMAZ ZELLEKE

BUILDING CLASS SOLIDARITY GLOBALLY

Sociologist Kim Scipes argues that we need to build solidarity among workers both locally and globally in order to tackle labour exploitation in a globalized world. We need to extend our understanding of solidarity beyond the nation state, connect exploitation at work to broader forms of domination and recognize global networks of power.

Strategies of global labour solidarity include struggles against:

- multinational or transnational corporations who exploit workers
- global or national political-economic plans that are detrimental to workers' interests
- militarism and invasion
- imperial activities

in order to:

- establish and maintain unions to improve working conditions
- improve the lives of workers outside of work in their communities
- support oppressed peoples
- liberate themselves
- protect workers from victimization through legal and political institutions.

In 2008, dock workers in Durban, organized by the South African Transport and Allied Workers Union, refused to unload weapons from a Chinese ship that were intended for Zimbabwe.

UTOPIA

Sociologist Ruth Levitas argues that by imagining a utopian society we can find ways to improve our current state. A utopia is an imagined society which is a good place for all citizens. Levitas suggests that imagining a utopia not only helps us understand what is wrong with our present society, but can help us think about society in a more holistic way.

We often formulate our critiques and reforms within the established framework, extrapolating the future from our current conditions. This means that we can ignore possible models of society that are outside of the accepted structures of global capitalism and the inequalities of the market. Rather than looking from the present to the future, the utopian method looks from an envisioned future to the present; first we imagine where we want to be, and then what steps we can take to get there.

ALTERNATIVE SOCIETIES

Sociologist Luke Martell argues that capitalist society fails to centre human needs, as we've seen in policies that only value citizens based on their ability to do paid labour. If we gradually introduce non-capitalist institutions and social arrangements (where people, services and materials are not reduced to objects of trade) we can take steps towards creating an alternative society.

Martell suggests that we can disrupt the dominance of capitalism by making small changes in our lives to how we work, where we live, how we learn and how we trade.

Work: Capitalism is based on high rates of production and consumption; we work to earn our wage in order to spend it on goods and services. But long hours, intensive work and a lack of control over our labour is not good for our health. We could have less paid work, which would have the environmental benefits of disrupting the cycle of production and consumption and give us more time to pursue autonomous work and non-work activities.

Housing: Community land trusts collectively own and manage homes and other assets such as farms and renewable energy systems. They are non-profit organizations which aim to make homes affordable by protecting the cost of housing from fluctuations in the housing market. Community land trusts can only sell or develop their assets in a way which benefits the local community.

PLAY PARK

COMMUNITY CENTRE

WIND TURBINE

LIBRARY

PUB

GYM

WHAT DOES OUR COMMUNITY NEED?

HOW MUCH DO YOU WANT TO PAY FOR YOUR EDUCATION ??? £9000 £3000 £1000 FREE

CARD

Education: Free universities have developed in many countries in response to the marketization of Higher Education, which involves the university being run like a business, resulting in rising tuition fees and decreased control by students and staff. Free universities see education as a public good and are run co-operatively.

Trade: Mutual aid offers an alternative economic culture organized through community networks. Set up by self-organized volunteers, mutual aid groups facilitate the reciprocal exchange of goods and services, with the aim of supporting members of the community through sharing resources. The idea is that we can learn and share the skills and things we need to live – from growing food to caring for each other, creating places to live and passing on knowledge.

CHAPTER 9: CLASS IN OUR LIVES

In this book, we have pointed to a range of different ways of understanding and analyzing class. These have included exploring class in relation to production, resources, inequalities, culture, action, identities and experiences. Theories of class can help us to think about how the world around us is organized, how this impacts us and others, and what we can do about it.

IN THE COMING PAGES, WE'LL ENCOURAGE YOU TO REFLECT ON HOW CLASS HAS IMPACTED YOUR OWN LIFE, AND HOW YOU CAN CHALLENGE CLASS INEQUALITIES IN EACH ASPECT THAT WE'VE TALKED ABOUT IN THE BOOK SO FAR: LABOUR, LAND, CULTURE AND THE EVERYDAY.

EACH PAGE WILL POSE A SERIES OF QUESTIONS WITH EXAMPLES AND IDEAS FOR YOU TO THINK ABOUT PUTTING INTO PRACTICE.

YOUR CLASS POSITION

Those of a privileged class position don't often have to think about class. Think about the resources the upper and middle classes have access to as if they were oxygen: we don't really think about breathing until we run out of oxygen.

Those who don't have access to inherited resources may struggle to find a name for our experience which doesn't have negative associations. We might point to those who are worse off than us in order to feel "normal".

Reflecting on our own class position can help us to understand how the histories of class inequality shape individual biographies. Make a timeline which marks key moments in your life. Think about moments that might have been impacted by your access to resources, support and networks, such as education, work, housing, relationships and family.

For each key moment, ask yourself:

HOW DID I FEEL?

DID I FEEL INCLUDED OR EXCLUDED, COMFORTABLE OR UNCOMFORTABLE, EXCITED OR SCARED?

WAS THIS EXPECTED?

DID THE SAME THING HAPPEN TO FRIENDS I GREW UP WITH? WAS I THE FIRST PERSON IN MY FAMILY TO DO THIS?

WHAT ENABLED ME TO DO THIS?

WHAT THINGS DID I NEED? COULD I AFFORD EVERYTHING I NEEDED? WHO HELPED ME?

WHAT BARRIERS DID I FACE?

WHAT DID I FIND DIFFICULT? WERE SOME OPTIONS NOT POSSIBLE FOR ME? WAS I ABLE TO GET HELP?

LABOUR

Does my workplace have a union?

IF YES, JOIN AND WORK TOGETHER WITH COLLEAGUES TO IMPROVE YOUR WORKING CONDITIONS. IF NOT, COULD YOU SET ONE UP? COULD YOU SUPPORT PEOPLE ON STRIKE IN OTHER WORKPLACES?

Where do the things I buy come from?

THERE ARE LOTS OF WAYS TO PUT PRESSURE ON COMPANIES TO IMPROVE WORKING CONDITIONS. YOU COULD: SUPPORT GROUPS WHO ARE CAMPAIGNING FOR CHANGE, FIND OUT AND SHARE INFORMATION ON EXPLOITATION, USE PROTESTS TO TELL COMPANIES THAT YOU DO NOT ACCEPT POOR TREATMENT OF WORKERS.

Who do I pay for services? Which tasks do I pay for that I could do myself, and why?

IF YOU SHOP ONLINE, FIND OUT ABOUT WHAT IT'S LIKE TO WORK FOR THOSE COMPANIES — DO THEY ALLOW TRADE UNIONS? ARE PEOPLE ON ZERO-HOUR CONTRACTS? THINK ABOUT YOUR INTERACTIONS WITH DELIVERY AND RETAIL STAFF, HAIRDRESSERS AND CLEANERS. ENSURE THAT YOU TREAT THEM WITH RESPECT AND PAY FAIRLY. FIND OUT WHAT WORKERS IN THESE INDUSTRIES ARE CAMPAIGNING AROUND, AND SUPPORT THEIR DEMANDS.

LAND

What places am I able to go to outside of my home? Can I spend time in parks, squares and gardens for free? Are these public spaces accessible for everyone?

IF NOT, YOU COULD JOIN DISABILITY CAMPAIGN GROUPS TO DEMAND INCLUSIVE PUBLIC SPACES. YOU COULD OCCUPY PUBLIC SPACES TO CALL FOR COLLECTIVE CONTROL OF COMMON LAND.

MAKE OUR PARKS ACCESSIBLE FOR EVERYONE!

Who owns and controls the land in my local community?

SOME OF THIS INFORMATION IS BEING MAPPED OUT BY CAMPAIGNERS; YOU COULD START BY LOOKING INTO LOCAL PLACE NAMES TO SEE WHERE THESE COME FROM.

WHY ARE THERE NO SIDEWALKS HERE? LET'S SEE WHO OWNS THIS STRETCH OF LAND.

What type of tenure is my home? How does this impact my housing security, the control I have and how I feel about my home?

COULD YOU JOIN WITH OTHERS TO FIGHT FOR FAIR ACCESS TO GOOD HOUSING? YOU COULD PARTICIPATE IN RENTERS UNIONS, RESIDENTS ASSOCIATIONS AND HOUSING CAMPAIGNS.

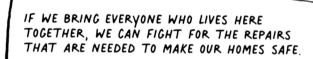

IF WE BRING EVERYONE WHO LIVES HERE TOGETHER, WE CAN FIGHT FOR THE REPAIRS THAT ARE NEEDED TO MAKE OUR HOMES SAFE.

CULTURE

What films, TV shows and news channels do I watch? Do prominent people in the media share the same background as me? Are people like me shown in a fair way? Or are people like me the only ones shown in a fair way?

FIND OUT ABOUT WHO OWNS AND PRODUCES DIFFERENT FORMS OF MEDIA. SUBSCRIBE TO FACT-CHECKED INDEPENDENT MEDIA. JOIN CAMPAIGNS FOR FAIRER REPRESENTATION.

THEY'RE WAY TOO POLITICAL FOR ME.

I CAN'T BELIEVE YOU WATCH THAT RUBBISH!

I DON'T TRUST THE TIMES.

DON'T YOU KNOW THEY'RE OWNED BY THE SAME COMPANY?!

What genres of music and fashion are important to me?

LOOK INTO THE HISTORY OF WHERE THEY COME FROM. IS A BIG CORPORATION PROFITING BY REPLICATING AND SELLING CULTURAL TRADITIONS? THINK ABOUT WHAT MEANING YOU ATTACH TO CULTURAL ITEMS AND PRACTICES AND WHAT MEANINGS THEY MIGHT HAVE FOR OTHER PEOPLE IN DIFFERENT CONTEXTS.

EDUCATION

What type of education did I have? How have my experiences at school shaped my life?

YOU COULD CHALLENGE CLASS HIERARCHIES IN EDUCATION BY JOINING CAMPAIGNS TO ABOLISH PRIVATE FEE-PAYING SCHOOLS AND DEMAND FREE HIGHER EDUCATION.

EVERYDAY

What communities do I feel part of? Do I ever feel excluded? How do I participate in my community?

THINK ABOUT HOW YOU COULD CONNECT WITH PEOPLE IN YOUR COMMUNITY. YOU COULD START UP CONVERSATIONS WITH YOUR NEIGHBOURS, GO ALONG TO COMMUNITY EVENTS OR GET INVOLVED IN LOCAL CAMPAIGNS OR POLITICAL PARTIES.

Do I feel connected to other communities across localities and borders?

YOU COULD GET INVOLVED IN ENVIRONMENTAL, ANTI-WAR, MIGRANT SOLIDARITY OR ANTI-POLICE-VIOLENCE WORK.

How do I feel about my class identity? Have I ever felt judged because of my class? Have I ever judged someone else because of their class?

THINK ABOUT THE LANGUAGE THAT YOU USE TO TALK ABOUT CLASS GROUPS AND THE IMPACT THIS HAS. YOU CAN CHALLENGE PEOPLE WHO USE DEROGATORY TERMS AND QUESTION CLASS STEREOTYPES.

I JUST DON'T THINK YOUNG GIRLS ARE READY FOR CHILDREN, THEY JUST IGNORE THEM AND WANT TO HANG OUT WITH THEIR FRIENDS.

ISN'T THAT EXACTLY WHAT WE'RE DOING TOO?

What does friendship mean to me? In what ways am I similar or different to my friends? How do I help my friends and in what ways do they support me? What kind of resources are available to me through my friendship networks?

THINK ABOUT WHO YOU ARE DRAWN TO AS FRIENDS. ARE THERE PLACES/GROUPS WHERE YOU MIGHT MEET DIFFERENT PEOPLE? IF YOU HAVE ACCESS TO RESOURCES, THINK ABOUT HOW YOU MIGHT SHARE THESE MORE WIDELY.

WE WENT BACKPACKING TOGETHER.

I HELPED YOU GET YOUR FIRST JOB.

YOU CALL ME WHEN YOU'RE UPSET.

WE BOUGHT OUR FIRST FLAT TOGETHER.

I INTRODUCED YOU TO YOUR PARTNER.

FURTHER RESOURCES

We hope that this introduction has sparked your interest to find out more about social class, and inspired you to read and listen to the writers who have appeared throughout the book.

Please remember that speech bubbles should not be read as direct quotes – they often present paraphrased text to give a sense of that individual's ideas, rather than their exact words.

Here are some resources you could look at that explore social class in more detail.

Introductions to social class
Bottero, W. (2004) *Stratification: Social Division and Inequality*. Routledge.
Savage, M. (2015) *Social Class in the 21st Century*. Pelican.

Theoretical books
Back, L. (2007) *The Art of Listening*. Bloomsbury.
Bhattacharya, T. (Ed) (2017) *Social Reproduction Theory: Remapping Class, Recentering Oppression*. Pluto Press.
hooks, b. (2000) *Where we stand: class matters*. Routledge.
Skeggs, B. (2004) *Class, Self, Culture*. Taylor & Francis.

Think tank and NGO reports
Eurofound and International Labour Organization (2019) *Working Conditions in a Global Perspective*. Publications Office of the European Union, Luxembourg, and International Labour Organization, Geneva.

Kham, O. and Shaheen, F. (Eds) (2017) *Minority Report: Race and Class in Post-Brexit Britain*. Runnymede Trust.

Taking action
Sisters Uncut Toolkit:
http://www.sistersuncut.org/wp-content/uploads/2016/02/SU_Toolkit.pdf

Staying Put: An Anti-Gentrification Handbook for Council Estates in London
https://justspacelondon.files.wordpress.com/2014/06/staying-put-web-version.pdf

Training for Change: resources for grassroots organizing:
https://www.trainingforchange.org/

ACKNOWLEDGEMENTS

Sarah and Laura would like to thank Kiera Jamison, Yaa Asare, Gillian Love, Reuben Bard-Rosenberg, Tansy Hoskins and Hanna Milner for support with the writing.

In addition, Sarah would like to thank Benjamin Marent for sharing his encyclopedic knowledge of sociology and David Davies for his daily insights on the workings of class.

Laura would like to thank Ema Webb and the writing collective at the Centre for Transforming Sexuality and Gender in Brighton, as well as Meg-John Barker and Kanwal Mand.

Danny would like to thank Laura and Sarah for letting her join their gang, Hanna and Kiera for being so supportive, and all the good comrades campaigning for a fairer world.

BIOGRAPHIES

Sarah Leaney is a sociologist at the University of Brighton. Her research explores class, community and council estates. She has published work on class inequalities in housing and education.

Laura Harvey is a feminist sociologist who works at the University of Brighton. Her work looks at gender, sexuality, youth and media. She has co-authored two other books: *Mediated Intimacy: Sex Advice in Media Culture* with Meg-John Barker and Rosalind Gill, and *Celebrity, Aspiration and Contemporary Youth: Education and Inequality in an era of Austerity*, with Heather Mendick, Kim Allen and Aisha Ahmad.

Danny Noble is an illustrator and writer. She has illustrated children's books written by Adrian Edmondson, published a graphic memoir, *Shame Pudding*, and won a Comedy Women in Print Award for her comic *Was It...Too Much For You?*.